EXECUTING WITH EXCELLENCE

... the pathway for outstanding performance

Jamie Pajoel

COPYRIGHT PAGE.

EXECUTING WITH EXCELLENCE

Published by Max-Living Publishers, a subsidiary of Max-Living Incorporated, Nigeria.
www.maxlivinginc.com

Table of Contents

ABOUT THE AUTHOR

JAMIE PAJOEL, APMC, ACBMP,

Venture Capitalist and Global Business Leader, Jamie Pajoel is the President of Legislative Leadership Education, Canada, and CEO of Vantage Group–a multi-million investment group of companies comprising Vantage Heights Capital, Vantage Canadian College, Vantage Studios, Vantage Consulting and Vantage Certifications.

As a Global Leadership and Management Consultant, he consults for Government Institutions and provides training to Top Governments officials, Captains of industries, Senior Executives, Managing Directors, and Senior and Middle-Level Managers from different organizations across the globe. Jamie Pajoel is a brand name in the field of Leadership and Management Consultant and is making waves internationally with many ideas on Organizational Leadership, simplifying processes, identifying underlying problems in Business and addressing ineffective Leadership practices, all of which can create dysfunctional systems, if ignored.

He is the author of 'Executing with Excellence', 'Building Strong Institutions', 'Leading From Within', and 'Less Is More'. As a Leadership and Management expert with experience in designing, implementing and managing corporate training which fosters Human Capital Development, his approach offers innovative methods for gaining employee commitment to organizational objectives. It incorporates real case studies and practical applications that support managing diverse personalities and an in-depth understanding of why the human experience approach is critical to organizational success. Jamie Pajoel is a recipient of the State of Michigan Leadership Award in the United States of America and a delegate to President Bill Clinton's program in the United States of America.

As an international keynote speaker, Jamie Pajoel has delivered speeches, as well as attended Leadership programs at Johns Hopkins University; Carey Business School, Baltimore, Maryland; African Union Headquarters, Ethiopia; U.S Embassy, Abuja, Nigeria and World Bank Summit, Washington DC, U.S.A.

Jamie Pajoel is the founder of J.P.I (Jamie Pajoel International) an NGO with a vision to support over one thousand families under the J.P.I FAMILY SUPPORT PROGRAM, provides education scholarships through JPI EDUCATION SCHOLARSHIPS, provides access to global opportunities through JPI GLOBAL EXCHANGE PROGRAM and support young entrepreneurs to gain access to funding through JPI ENTERPRISE GRANT AWARD.

ABOUT THE BOOK

This book is the product of the journey into a life committed to the relentless pursuit of excellence and the impact it has had on my personal and professional life.

It is my sincere and genuine desire to share these lessons with the world. My greatest joy and challenge as a global Leadership and Corporate trainer is my charge to instil in each member of my audience the hunger, passion, and respect for the process that excellence requires. Some people make excuses not to do the things necessary to achieve excellence. They look for shortcuts, and ways to beat the system and lack a sense of accountability for their results.

This book is about accomplishing all undertakings and day-to-day endeavours with excellence. It will help you blaze new trails, become the best version of yourself and develop a zero tolerance for mediocrity. It is about refusing to settle for less by constantly raising the standards and expectations for yourself and those you lead.

Why aspire for more when your work is good enough? Remember that "good enough" is a mindset just as "excellence" is. When an individual becomes satisfied with the "good enough" mindset, the traits of complacency, mediocrity, and apathy slowly become the habits that shape their work and lives.

DEDICATION

**This book is dedicated
To**

....

By

....

**On the occasion
Of**

....

Date

....

PREFACE

My journey has carried me miles away from the street to some corridors of power. It was while I was at a function with President Bill and Hillary Clinton foundation in New York that I had an epiphany.

In retrospect, I can draw similarities between some principles that enabled me to excel as a street hawker and become a global business and leadership coach.

Through my experiences, I can confidently say that excellence is a mindset. It's a way of doing things and the underlying force that shaped the experiences I've had on either front.

The book in your possession is my shot at exposing you to the world of excellent thinking, excellent talking and excellent doing!

INTRODUCTION

"Starting today, let's banish the philosophy of mediocrity. No matter your occupation or endeavour, you and your people (team members) must create excellence on your turf. It can be done, and it is done. There is no excuse for not getting on with it among your people".

Tom Peters.

YOUR LIFE

Chapter 1: Making Things Work

Today, I have the privilege of sharing my ideas and knowledge with you through this book, which I believe you encountered because of your desire to grow in knowledge.

I also know that you want more no matter where you are in your life. No matter how challenging your life and business are, deep within you lies a belief that it can be much better than it already is.

You do not only believe that, but you are also doing something right now that fortunately is unique—you are reading this book! Statistics show that less than 10 per cent of people who buy a book read past the first chapter. What an unbelievable waste.

This book will unveil deep understandings to you. So, I

challenge you not only to do whatever it takes to ensure you complete reading it but also to utilize whatever you learn herein to add value to yourself and the people around you.

When it comes to making things work, too often, people think they cannot do it. Even athletes like Serena Williams inspire us to change our ideas about the limits of what is possible or impossible. Most people do not try to do it because they think they cannot, even when they can. All they need to do is change channels from why they cannot to why they can.

At the time, breaking the barrier of running a sub-4-minute mile was viewed as impossible, until an athlete did it. And almost immediately, a host of others did it, because they knew it was possible.

These runners' physical and technical skills did not change per se; what changed was their belief—from the impossibility to possibility.

Cars were impossible, aeroplanes were impossible, space travel was impossible, and hundreds of other things were impossible at one time or the other until some inventors "decided" to make them possible.

As our beliefs about our limits and unlimited possibilities change, limits change in all parts of our society and all aspects of life. The world's best performers in all disciplines are made of the same flesh and blood as you and me, but their belief is different;

their focus is different; their commitment is different; their passion is different; their persistence is different. That is what gives them their strength.

Almost anything is possible whenever you focus on positive possibilities. Your positive focus, commitment, and belief in your capacity will birth new and better realities.

Have you ever done anything that you initially thought was impossible to do? Have you ever thought, "I am never going to be able to do this," "I am not going to be successful with this," "I am never going to finish this," or "There is no way this is going to work," "There is no way I can win this," yet you and your partner or team were successful?

You and your partner (or team) accomplished a goal that initially seemed impossible. Most people have thought, at least momentarily, that they cannot do something but then managed to do it at last. It is simply because they were able to shift focus. They shifted away from their doubts and connected fully with doing what they wanted to do and were capable of doing.

Can you recall a personal experience when this happened to you? If you can, think about how you or your team managed to achieve your goal when you initially thought you could not. What did you focus or refocus on to make it happen?

It is important to take time to reflect on the moments

in which you were most focused and least focused. And, remember what you did to turn negatives into positives or impossible into possible.

Every year, there are teams or individual athletes who are not supposed to win. Yet, they defeat their opponents who are highly rated to win. How do you think they do this? They usually win or raise the level of their performance because they centre their individual or collective focus on the right things at the right time.

You can achieve the impossible when you commit to focusing on achieving your mission and attaining your goals step by step, and from beginning to end.

Athletes and other professionals that perform at their absolute best are almost always so focused on improving what they know how to do. They free themselves to do it. They do not allow doubts or distracting thoughts to get in their way of achieving their positive mission.

I have trained thousands of individuals and corporate organizations worldwide on personal and professional development. I can say that most people are unbelievably ambivalent about how to make the right decisions to move their organizations forward.

People want to scale up. They are working very hard, but they are just not breaking through. They desire to go for their dreams, yet they are afraid they will be judged as crazy or fail if they try. Additionally, the unrelenting tasks, the self-doubt, the unwanted obligations, the overwhelming choices and the responsibilities are enough to exhaust anyone. Some too many people believe that things will never get better. Such people always swim in a churning sea of distractions and disappointments. If that sounds dire, it is.

Most people are hopeful and ready to make a change but lack direction and the right habits. Whenever this happens, they risk living unexciting, disconnected, and unfulfilling lives. Of course, many people are living happy and wonderful lives. However, consistency is a problem.

They may feel capable—even feel that they hit "peak performance" occasionally—but there's always that cliff on the other side. And so, people are tired of the ups and downs of peak performance.

They are wondering how to reach a sustainable level of growth and success. They do not need only new tricks to get into better states and moods; they need real skills and methods to holistically advance their lives and careers.

My entire life has been continually driven by a singular compelling focus: What makes the difference in the quality of people's lives? How is it that so often people from such humble beginnings and devastating backgrounds manage despite their hardships to create lives that inspire us? What makes some people living examples and others a warning? What is the secret that creates passionate, happy and grateful lives in many? What precedes all our actions? What determines what action we take? Whom do we become? What our ultimate destination is in life?

At an early age, I realized that I was here to contribute something unique; I had a great desire to impact lives. It spoke to me each morning; it kept me up at night pondering about it. But, I could not find the answer to it.

I had a desire to fulfil my dream, and live happily and freely. Just ahead of me was a very colourful future, a height I wished to reach, a dream I wished to attain, a mission I wished to accomplish, and a vision I wished to achieve. It was indeed an assignment I ought to carry out. Yet, I could not find the answer to it.

Well, observing other humans appeared that most of them had found the secret to living their dreams and making things work for their good. Yet others (like me) were still living by default, believing it could not be done.

All my life, I did not understand the difference between being poor and being broke. Social conditioning had made me believe that money was the only capital I needed to achieve success in life. Perhaps, I had that inordinate mindset because I was not born into a rich family. Thus, I concluded that I was not a candidate for greatness.

This decision to become a person of value is what I often refer to as a great turning point in my life. This turning point brought about a positive transformation in who I am and the way I currently live my life. It turned my negative, closed mindset into a broad, positive and open approach to life.

I stopped living by default and started living life by design. I minimized complaining about what life brings me and focused on what my life brings to others. I became more practical in what I do for others and conscious of what goes into my mind. I became more aware that I can accomplish a lot with the little I have—it is all about perspective.

This understanding changed my life. Consequently, I decided that I would invest in developing my mind. I decided that, somehow, I must focus on BECOMING a person of value.

It is a simple equation. The more valuable you are, the more successful you become. Also, bear in mind that value and influence are connected. The value grows when influence grows.

This story may not be described with minute accuracy, but its sum and substance are correct. DECISION MAKING was all I needed to live my dreams.

Virtually everything you do or do not do in your life is ruled by the choices you make—ditto the actions you take or do not take. You can choose to excel or choose not to. You can choose to bring a positive and fully connected focus into what you do or choose not to. You can choose to be negative or stressed out about things beyond your control or choose not to.

You can choose to let other people's comments, actions, or inactions upset you or choose not to. You can choose to approach obstacles or challenges in positive ways or negative ways.

You can choose to dwell on the negatives that drag you down or focus on the positives that can lift your spirit and give you positive energy. You can choose to embrace your dreams and pursue them with total focus or let them drift away without really trying.

These are *your choices*, and your choices direct the quality and consistency of your performance as well as how joyful your life is. You decide for better or worse.

Take a quick look over the last five years. Were there times when a different decision would have made your life radically different from today, either for better or worse? Maybe you made a career decision that changed your life or maybe you failed to make one. Maybe you attended a conference, and it changed your beliefs and actions. How has your decision brought you to this point in your life?

The decisions that you are making right now, every day, will shape how you feel today as well as the person you are going to become in the future.

You can make your life count if you decide to. How? Simply by making decisions today about how you are going to live your life. If you do not make decisions about how you live, then you have decided already.

Haven't you? You have decided to be directed by the environment instead of shaping your destiny. If you do not make decisions about what you will accept in your life, you will find it easy to slip into behaviours and attitudes or a quality of life that is far below what you deserve.

You need to make decisions by which you will live your life going forward regardless of what happens in your life. Decide right now. Even if it all goes wrong, even if it rains, even if the stock market crashes, even if no one gives you the support that you need, you still must stay committed to your decisions—that you will live a quality life at the highest level.

Unfortunately, most people never do this because they are too busy making excuses. Perhaps, they have not achieved their goals or are not living the lives they desire because of the way their parents treated them, because of the lack of opportunities that they experienced, or because they are too young. All these excuses are nothing but limiting and they are destructive.

Using the power of decision enables you to instantly get past any excuse to change any and every part of your life. It can change your income and state of mind. It can determine whether you are happy or sad, whether you are free or bound. It is the source of change within an individual.

You certainly do not have to do what you have done for the last five years. You can decide to do something new today. Right now, you can decide to go back to school, to master dancing or singing, to take control of your life.

If you do not like the status quo in your life, decide to change it right now. If you do not like your current job, change it. If you dislike the way you feel about yourself, change it. You can make a new decision right now that can change your life—a decision about a habit you will change or a skill that you will master, or a call that you will make to someone you have not spoken to in years.

True decisions catalyze our dreams into reality. The most exciting thing about this force is that you already possess it. The explosive impetus of decision is not something reserved for a select few with the right credentials, money or family background.

It is available to the common labourer as well as the king. It's available to you now as you hold this book. In this very next moment, you can use this force that lies within you. All you need is to muster the courage to claim it.

Will today be the day you finally decide that you are much more than what you have been demonstrating?

Will today be the day you decide once and for all to make your life count?

Many people are paralyzed by the fear that they do not know exactly how to turn their dreams into reality. Ipso facto they never make the decisions that will transform their lives into the masterpieces they deserve to be. The "how" will reveal itself if you simply decide what you want in life.

If making decisions is so simple and powerful, then why don't more people decide to just do it? I think one of the simplest reasons is that most of us do not recognize what it means to make a real decision.

We do not realize the force of change that a committed decision creates. Part of the problem is that most of us have used the term "decision" so loosely for so long that it has now been reduced to a mere wish list. We keep stating preferences instead of making decisions.

I could have easily chosen any other available career when I voluntarily opted for my line of profession many years ago as a leadership coach. But I made up my mind because of my unflinching passion for it. I was committed to my decision; I was conscious of my actions.

Making a true decision, unlike saying, "I'd like to quit procrastination," is cutting off any other possibility. You will never procrastinate again when you truly decide. That is it. It is over! You will no longer even consider the possibility of doing it.

You will know exactly what I am talking about if you are one of the people who exercise the power of decision this way. After making a true decision, even a tough one, most of us feel tremendously relieved. And, I am sure you know how great it feels to have a clear, a

With true decisions, you can produce the results you want for your life. Interestingly, the only way to make better decisions is to make more of them. Then, you learn from each one, including those that do not seem to work out in your life. They will provide valuable distinctions to make better evaluations and decisions in the future.

Realize that decision-making, like any other skill you want to improve, gets better the more often you do it. The more decisions you make, the more you will realize that you truly are in control of your life. The three decisions that will determine your future are what you will notice, how you will feel, and ultimately whom you will become in life.

You are not in control of your life if you do not control these three decisions. It is not what happens to you now or what has happened in your past that determines whom you become. Rather, it is your decision about what to focus on, what things mean to you, and what you are going to do about them that determine your future.

Know that if anyone is enjoying greater success than

you in any area, they are making these decisions differently from you in some manner. But, you do not need to worry. With this book, you can reinvest in yourself by systematically organizing your beliefs and values in a way that pulls you in the direction of your life's dream.

There is one final impediment to utilizing the power of decision: the fear of making wrong decisions. You must overcome your fear of making the wrong decisions. You will undoubtedly make wrong decisions in your life. You are going to screw up. Fact!

I certainly have not made all the right decisions along the way, nor will I always make the right decisions in the future. Albeit, I have determined that no matter what decisions I make, I will be flexible, look at the consequences, learn from them, and use those lessons to make better decisions in the future.

There will be times when you are on a river solo, and you will have to make some important personal decisions. Any extremely successful person you meet will tell you (if they are honest) that they are successful because they have made more poor decisions than you have.

People often ask me, "How long do you think it will take me to master this particular decision-making skill?" My immediate response is always, "How long do you want it to take"? I try to tell them what I am telling you now—making things work takes as long as you want it to take.

Stay committed to your decisions but stay flexible in your approach.
Once you have decided whom you want to be as a person, do not get stuck on the means to achieving it. Too often, people pick the best way they know at the time but then do not stay open to alternate routes. Finally, I want you to remember that everything you read in this book is worthless unless you decide to put it to good use.

Chapter 2: Mindset of Excellence

Over the past ten years, I have conducted several leadership-related personnel workshops for many organizations. Very few of these organizations have demonstrated the spirit I always look out for.

So, what distinguishes excellent companies from merely good ones? The answer lies not in what you see, or the tools they use, but in the feel, the pure essence of these organizations.

It is the mindset, the language, the confidence and the sheer passion for excellence. In the following pages, we will explore what I have learned.

I have developed a framework for our thinking. I hope to inspire and guide you in your search for excellence.

Excellence begins with our mindset. There is no other way to achieve it. If repetition is required for mastery, mindset is required for achievement. Human beings do not act if they do not believe in something.

Mental readiness refers to a positive state you carry into learning and performance situations. It depends on the other mental skills on the **Wheel of Excellence**, which we will talk about later.

To have a realistic chance of excelling, you must become highly proficient at mentally preparing yourself to do these few things: learn essential mental, physical and technical skills, and practice and effectively perform those skills under competitive conditions.

Personal excellence requires that you become proficient at getting the most out of your daily learning and living experiences. This begins with a commitment to make the most of each testing experience and performance. Excellence demands that you consistently develop an effective way to enter a high-quality, focused, performance zone.

You need an effective mental plan that maximizes your state of readiness for learning and performance. Positive images and thoughts, specific reminders about what you want to do and how you can focus best are normally incorporated into this mental readiness process.

You must be open to learning and committed to ongoing personal growth if you want to excel at learning, performing, and living. You must engage yourself in a continuous process of self-discovery. More importantly, act upon those discoveries that aid your primary focus and best performance. Your focus is the lead. Once you discover what works best, you must follow that path, even in the face of obstacles from others who may dictate or suggest another path.

Consistent high-level performers are great at following their own best path. They carry a positive perspective, respect what works best for them, focus and continue to look for ways to improve. This path becomes so natural for some great performers that they can follow it consistently without much conscious awareness.

The quality of your life is the reflection of your standards. You could make millions and still stay poor in your mind. Being poor is not about making less money. Being poor is a mentality; it is a choice to live a low standard of life that is characterized by an individual's inability to recognize abundance.

When I say low standard, I am not equating standards to the financial capacity of the rich versus the poor but people's frame of mind. You can raise your standards regardless of how much money you make.

Think for a moment, would you jump out of an aeroplane without knowing that you would not hit the ground and die? That is the same thing with achievement. Would you jump into an entrepreneurial career without believing? Nobody would do that unless he/she is crazy. The mindset of excellence is accompanied by an irrefutable belief that success is guaranteed if an endeavour is carried out with excellence.

So, if success is tied to a mindset, how can an individual create a mindset of excellence that can allow him/her to focus and follow the path of success relentlessly?

The answer lies in understanding that the mindset for excellence is hinged on a decision to be the best and to do what it takes to honour this decision. Therefore, excellence is intentional. It is not born with you, but it is not something you cannot reach. You can choose whether to have it or not—it is up to you.

Being the best isn't a matter of luck, but something accomplished intentionally, through investment. — Jamie Pajoel

If you are determined to be the best, your new excellence mentality will start producing excellent thoughts. Thoughts of self-confidence, faith and success, such as "I can do it," "I'll succeed in everything I do" and "Today, I must be better off than yesterday." Then, you will develop the characteristics you need for God to use you in greater ways.

As success magazine, founder and thought leader Orison Swett Marden states, "Just make up your mind at the very outset that your work is going to stand for quality ... that you are going to stamp a superior quality upon everything that goes out of your hands; that whatever you do shall bear the hallmark of excellence."

Do those words inspire you? They certainly inspire me! I believe executing with excellence is a noble goal in anything you do. It is a wonderful way to live your life and provides a constant source of motivation and inspiration. Sometimes, we achieve it, and sometimes we fall short, but we will not have any regrets if we always work towards it.

Excellence is compelling, in part, because it is hard to achieve. The philosopher Plato even said, "Excellent things are rare." But sometimes, excellence is not expected. Sometimes the bar is not very high. Sometimes good enough is good enough. But, for those who aspire to greatness, good enough is not enough. So, what does excellence look like? Why should we pursue it? And, what values must we master to achieve it?

Chapter 3: Raise the Bar—It's time to play the A-game

It is always a pleasure to meet new people. However, if individuals aren't careful about the people they surround themselves with, such individuals may get stuck in a mediocre or stereotypical thinking pattern because humans are products of their associations. You must make a conscious decision not to lower your standards to fit into that of other people simply because of association.

"Refuse to lower your standards to accommodate those who refuse to raise theirs." — Mandy Hale
Watch out for the people who show jealousy, selfishness, passive aggression, dishonesty, or narcissism. You need to surround yourself with people

who accept, respect and inspire you to become better. The people you choose to surround yourself with should inspire you in one way or another, despite their inadequacies or imperfection.

Understand that each person is different and has flaws. Despite this, you must learn to accept people, especially if they help you grow and are compatible with you.

You get a better outcome when you raise your work standards and because of this undying passion, you will love your work. Average work leads to lousy results, and that is when we hate our work.

"We only get what we believe that we deserve. Raise the bar, raise your standards and you will receive a better outcome." — Joel Brown

When you commit to raising the bar constantly, you will not be shattered by your failures or setbacks. Raising the bar also means you have raised the standard of your mindset to a level that does not recognize failures as fatal. You will see obstacles as an opportunity to learn and grow. You will get inspired instead of getting jealous and you will participate in healthy competition instead of comparing yourself with others.

I recommend that you identify where you lack standards and zealously raise the bar. Think about the cost and consequences of not raising your standards. Change your limiting beliefs and take measurable actions to silence self-doubt. Raising your standards is not about being an egomaniac. It is about having a healthy level of self-respect.

You need to develop a strong work ethic, keep your commitments and over-deliver to stand out from the crowd. Find your strengths and develop them to add value to the world.

The winds of change through technology have made average work obsolete as machines are currently replacing average. Develop creativity and great thinking skills to secure your place in the future workforce.

You raise your standards every time you ignore the lizard brain, say no to distractions, delayed gratification or choose voluntary discomfort. Daily small choices set the foundation for your standards. Stop reacting to temptations.

The urge to open social media, check notifications, eat unhealthy meals, skip workouts, buy unnecessary stuff, dwell on the past, or waste time will always be there. You must recognize them and kill them before they kill you.

Temptations are very misleading. They seek momentary pleasure and disregard the future. You do not have to act on your urges. Making the right decisions in the wake of strong urges is a sign of true wisdom. When you are faced with urges, acknowledge them, and do the right thing anyway. You will feel proud, and your self-confidence will become unshakable.

You do not have to give up all the pleasures in life. You can enjoy pleasurable experiences in moderation. Find a healthy balance for yourself but do not indulge beyond your allowance.

Your thoughts determine your actions. If you want to put quality thoughts in your mind, you must craft your environment in a way that most thoughts in your mind are useful or helpful.

Destructive patterns lead to depression, worry or anxiety. Your internal self-talk is the way to communicate with your subconscious. Make sure you talk to yourself from a higher perspective.

Become your life coach. Use the power of self-affirmation to feel powerful and inspired to become great. Most people never recognize what they are capable of because they think too small and lack self-efficacy.

Take inspiration from mentors or the best work in your field and add your touch to create the best work you can now. Your work will only improve if you set high expectations for yourself. This, however, should not stop you from shipping your craft because quantity brings quality.

Sometimes, you will find that your current standards

are lower than your desired standards. That is okay as long as you recognize the gap and work better to reduce the gap. Run your race and continually create, learn, reflect and improve. Eliminate all the excuses.

Take full responsibility for your life. You know you are on the path of growth when you're working to raise your future standards and when your present ideals are higher than your past standards. Below are the habits you must develop in your pursuit of excellence.

Hunger
Hunger is the first habit you must develop if you are going to work towards excellence. Hunger in this context is a desire to achieve excellence. Hunger is an intrinsic quality, and it is up to you as an individual to fend for yourself.

"When you are hungry, you don't wait to be served."
Jamie Pajoel.

If you are not hungry, if you are not passionate, if you do not want to excel and succeed, do not worry—you will not. If you do, if you genuinely want to achieve something significant, you can, but you must be hungry.

Think about it this way, if you go into a restaurant with the wrong attitude, "I'm not hungry," "There is nothing here I want to eat," or "I don't want to be here," the menu most likely is not going to look appealing. You will not explore it with enthusiasm, and it is unlikely you will find a cuisine which you will enjoy eating. Ditto for your work. If you go to work each day expecting to be bored and uninspired, that is exactly what your reality will become.

You will remain closed to possibilities if you are convinced that it is hard to execute with excellence, or that it is not going to happen for you. You will block the little nudges, pulls, and signals that guide us all. After all, how can you expect to execute with excellence if you do not believe in it?

Not only must you want excellence, but you must also be willing to earn it. And even more importantly, you must be eager to do whatever is necessary (legally) to accomplish your goal.

Hunger helps push you through the tough times and inevitable adversity that will accompany your road to greatness.

Hunger for excellence strengthens your perseverance, persistence, and sacrifice. It is simply essential for making things happen. Hunger exhibitors have these four characteristics:
1. They are proactive.
2. They begin with the end in mind.
3. They are self-motivated.
4. They exhibit desire.

Let us take a closer look at these characteristics vis-à-vis your hunger for excellence.

Hunger is also about passion. Without question, hunger is one of the keys to success in any endeavour. We are positive, hopeful, and energized when we are hungry for something. We are inflated rather than deflated.

I believe that the feeling of anticipation, having something to look forward to, is one of the best feelings in the world. It could be a vacation, a date, a big performance or a presentation. Or, it could be waiting to hear if your book will be published, if you were accepted into college, or if you got the new job you applied for.

Hunger is all about the desire and passion for wanting to be successful and this feeling of anticipation fills us with reservoirs of energy that enable us to continue working towards excellence. When you are hungry for real success, you will realize that your appetite craves excellence, and nothing less will satisfy you when you decide to make that decision.

Begin with the End in Mind
The second habit of highly effective people, according to Covey, is to "Begin with the End in Mind." This habit is incontrovertibly one of the most significant differences between successful and unsuccessful people. To begin with the end in mind effectively, an individual must be proactive in establishing a game plan and work backwards, visualizing the result and working towards excellence daily.

Become Self-Motivated

As a trainer, I believe one of my responsibilities is to motivate my students. I must get them excited about executing with excellence, and precision, and working towards fulfilling their dreams. I engage my students by inspiring them through my passion, believing in them, and challenging them to reach their zenith.

Most importantly, I teach them to develop a hunger for excellence and achievement. I encourage them to become self-motivated and not depend on others for motivation.

Intrinsic motivation is the ability to motivate oneself. Intrinsic motivation means being motivated by interest or gratification in the task itself. It exists within an individual—independent of any external force.

Conversely, extrinsic motivation originates from an individual's external environment. Rewards such as money, grades, coercion, and punishments are all common extrinsic motivations.

Competition falls in the general extrinsic motivation category because it inspires the performer to win, outperform other competitors, and not enjoy the intrinsic rewards inherent in the activity.

My mentor taught me the value of competition and how to become self-motivated to achieve excellence. From that point forward, I made up my mind not to allow judgments, people or things outside my control to motivate me. Instead, I persist in finding the motivation within myself.

Unseen intrinsic drive is the secret to high performance —the drive to do things because they matter.
I believe this drive comprises three elements:
1. Autonomy
2. Mastery
3. Purpose

Autonomy has to do with the desire to direct our own lives. Mastery is our urge to get better and better at something that matters, and purpose is the yearning buried deep within us, spurring us to do the things we do in the service of something larger than ourselves.

YOUR WORK

Chapter 4: In Pursuit of Excellence

The psychological barriers we often unconsciously impose on others and ourselves constitute the greatest obstacles in the pursuit of personal and performance excellence. No matter what you do in life, doing it well has a great reward. Whether this applies to your work, health, relationships, or goals, committing to personal excellence in whatever you do lays the foundation for a life of fulfilment, success and significance.

The quality and intensity of your effort are proportionate to the results you get. You will have meagre results if you discount excellence. You increase your chances of getting results (even if they are not what you initially intended) if you give your absolute best.

Do not confuse perfection with excellence. I do not need my pilot to land the aircraft perfectly—just safely! You cannot be a perfect leader because no rulebook tells you what is perfect. Does perfect mean everyone gets promoted or that everyone admires you? No, that will not happen, but you must be awesome at your level.

You must be filled with energy when you speak so that you light up the bulbs in everyone's minds. You want to stimulate people for emotional impact and give them gifts that they can use every day to be better at what they do—and balance it by working with the understanding that the pinnacle of great performance is excellence.

One reason people do not give their best effort is that they do not believe they are capable of more. Is this you? Do you avoid working harder than you have to? Do you believe there is no point in giving your best because success belongs to only the truly talented and lucky? You may be capable of achieving results 10 times more than you have achieved so far.

You are already working against reaching your peak if you do not believe you can do better. People improve when they believe they can perform better and are in control of their performance. You are already in the right mindset to change everything the moment you just consider that you can do better.

Think about your accomplishments and be realistic

with yourself about the things you could have done better. Perhaps, you avoided increased responsibility at your workplace and consequently lost your promotion, or you gave up on making your dream a reality because it seemed too difficult.

To bring out your excellence, you must first acknowledge that your present circumstances are typically due to your past actions or inactions. More importantly, the quality and intensity of your efforts are responsible for your present state.

Imagine you are in a shopping mall, standing before one of those "You are here" maps. You can easily map out a route to get somewhere else if you know where you are. Do not judge yourself guilty for your lack of accomplishment to date. Feeling disappointed can cause you to move decisively as well as take measured and focused action.

But for many, it accomplishes nothing. The point is to gain a clear understanding of where you are and figure out your next destination. Acknowledge that you did the best you could with the resources you had, but now you are ready to do better.

Defining Excellence

Excellence is the state or quality of surpassing a set of expectations or being outstandingly better. It is exceptional merit or a superlative performance or outcome. Essentially, excellence refers to anything related to being better than the rest.

Excellence is ...
Excellence is the best defence.
Excellence is the best offence.
Excellence is the answer in good times.
Excellence is the answer in tough times.
Excellence is about the big things.
Excellence is about the little things.
Excellence is a relationship.
Excellence is a philosophy.
Excellence is an aspiration.
Excellence is immoderate.
Excellence is a pragmatic standard.
Excellence is execution.
Excellence is selfish.
Excellence is selfless.
Excellence is what keeps you awake.
Excellence is what allows you to sleep well.
Excellence is a moving target.
Excellence is that which ... knows no bounds.
EXCELLENCE. always.
If not EXCELLENCE, what?
If not EXCELLENCE now, when?
EXCELLENCE is not an "aspiration."
EXCELLENCE is the next five minutes.
Excellence is not so much about what you do, but how you do it. The more time you spend doing things that matter to you, the more natural you will bring out your inner brilliance.

What is important to you?
What do you live for?

What have you always wanted to do?

Don't just skim through these questions while reading this book, pause to think critically of the answers as they pertain to you, because answering these questions will set you on an amazing journey of self-discovery and growth.

Once you know the activities that make your heart sing, do them often, and do them well. Master them as you have never mastered anything before. Throw yourself into them and become consumed by them. When you do something that you feel extremely passionate about, it enables you to automatically give the best of yourself to the task.

Being passionate about your endeavours helps you enjoy yourself more and lend much more power to the result. Partial effort begets lukewarm results while passionate action brings forth excellent results.

I know you have jobs, family responsibilities, mundane chores, and obligations. It is easy to slip into a mindset of drudgery and do these things with a half-hearted effort. You may do just that. But, what happens when you give them your full effort and attention? First, you feel immensely proud of yourself.

You will also feel good about the unpleasant tasks rather than feeling annoyed or weary. Sounds odd, but it is right.

I hate mechanical work, but I go for it. I can endure the stress that comes with it because it is a necessary component of my journey—and the accomplishment of such tasks feel good. Adapting to such aids the pursuit of excellence.

Second, you focus on the benefits created by the work you do, not the work itself. Third, you would gain a sense of personal mastery over just about everything you do: from errands to interpersonal relationships, each activity would feel like its own reward.

The results gained from these activities would simply be a nice bonus—a better organization, greater fulfilment, deeper relationships, and powerful results from projects.

Personal excellence creates a sense of inner pride about who you are and what you do. It makes you feel more confident, happy and focused. Commit to excellence in whatever you do. Do not clean out the garage because you "have to".

Do it as if it were the most important thing. Clean it out as if a neat garage is of utmost importance in the grand scheme of things. Clean it out as if you would rather be doing nothing else in the world.

Why does your attitude matter while performing a simple chore like cleaning out the garage? Three things will most likely happen if you approach any task with a sense of boredom or grudging obligation.

First, you will not enjoy the process at all. Your mind will focus only on getting it done, and you will not give full attention to what you are doing. Consequently, you will end up missing out on the enjoyment of the process. To make matters worse, you will be teaching your brain to become familiar with not going for things you do not like to do.

Second, your results would be less than stellar since you do not pay full attention to what you do. The garage might look "good," and you might be fine with that. But, wouldn't "better" be more desirable than "good"? The garage does not need to be surgical perfect; it needs to be better.

Third, with a ho-hum attitude, you could also miss out on the sense of accomplishment and satisfaction that comes from a job you do right. Perhaps, you think it does not matter because doing a job for its own sake is fine. Sometimes, that may be true.

However, it makes sense that you would want to enjoy the things you do, and experience better results from them if you want to experience greater fulfilment in your life. The only way to do that is to commit fully to everything you do.

Pay attention to it and allow yourself to become immersed in the process. Give it your absolute best and watch how it dramatically enhances your results!

Chapter 5: Wheel of Excellence

The wheel of excellence can free you to access incredible inner strength by directing the full power of your focus in positive and fully connected ways. You will immediately begin to add more quality and consistency to your performances and life if you strengthen the quality and consistency of your focus.

The wheel of excellence was created over many years of ongoing focused consulting, interviewing, learning, and interacting with some of the corporate leaders, coaches, and educators in different parts of the world who excelled in other challenging high-performance pursuits.

Some critical values guide the pursuit of personal and performance excellence in all positive human endeavours.

These five essential elements of excellence work together in positive and life-enhancing ways to create the wheel of human excellence. This integrated wheel of essential interconnected skills guides or drives the highest levels of excellence in every sport and other important human performance pursuits.

You can attain your absolute best and give yourself the best chance to achieve your dreams by "deciding" to embrace and improve all parts of the wheel of excellence.

You can improve the ongoing quality and consistency of your focus as well as your best performances by choosing to focus on improving any part of the wheel that you believe will benefit you and your performance. You are capable of strengthening any part of the wheel of excellence at any time and any age or stage of your development.

The Five Wheels of Excellence.

1. Commitment

The first element of excellence is your **COMMITMENT** to:

- Excel.
- Be the best you can be.
- Do everything required to excel.
- Develop the mental, physical and technical links to excellence.
- Set clear personal goals and relentlessly pursue them.
- Persist in the face of obstacles.
- Give everything of yourself you can.

Commitment is the first essential ingredient guiding the pursuit of excellence. You must have and develop an extremely high level of dedication, self-discipline, passion, joy or love for what you are doing to excel at anything. You must truly commit yourself to being the best and continuously strive to make personal improvements and meaningful contributions anywhere you are.

I have been fortunate to work with many corporate business leaders and learned many valuable lessons from each of them, which I have shared with others and applied to my life pursuits, including writing this book.

You must pursue excellence to achieve your full potential or live your dreams. Create or develop an underlying belief that you can do it. With big dreams and a full focus on embracing the little daily focused steps that will take you to where you want to go, you continue to nourish your long-term commitment, enhance your daily focus, strengthen your confidence, and give yourself good reasons to believe in yourself and your mission.

Even if you fall short of attaining your goal, your dream of getting there will still inspire you to become far better than you would have been. Most great and noble human accomplishments begin with a kind of positive vision or dream.

Every great human feat flashes through someone's mind before it surfaces as a concrete reality, whether it be flying to the moon; landing on Mars; becoming a great student, artist, writer, director, or In Pursuit of Excellence performer; making a positive difference in the world; healing *self*; excelling in a relationship; building a dynasty; or building a tree-house.

Positive dreams precede positive realities. Positive dreams nourish, direct, and even create positive realities. Our dreams of personal excellence, personal accomplishments, and meaningful contributions are forward reflections into a positive future.

A positive future makes us see ourselves fulfilling big dreams, being the way we want to be, and having the freedom to reach our desired destinations. Visions of excellence, creative accomplishment, and joyful and harmonious living are stimulating and uplifting.
They provide us with hope, meaningful positive

direction, and sustainable ongoing positive energy. Dreams of attaining our highest levels of personal and performance excellence often become memories of the future waiting to unfold, for those of us who choose to push beyond the occasional limitations of past and present experiences.

People who have excelled at anything had dreams of making a meaningful contribution, stretching their limits, accomplishing things important to them, becoming their best, or reaching their potential in their pursuits.

Successful people dream big and go after their dreams. They begin with a positive dream and focus on the step-by-step process of living or creating a better reality.

Some people dream big but do not act in concrete ways that will lead them to more positive new realities. Their lack of positive action is their essential disadvantage. Your dreams remain unachievable unless you act in positive ways every day to turn those dreams into positive living realities.

Some people remain stagnant because they do not dream of a better way, a better life, a better performance, or a higher level of humanity. Equally important, they do not act on their positive intentions because they do not believe in the possibility of living at a better or higher level.
But, we know people can turn things around by merely changing their impossible views to possible ones. Few

things are impossible when you believe strongly enough in the positive possibilities and focus on turning them into positive new realities.

Think about your dreams. Visit them often in your mind. Let them lead you. The best chance you have of moving forward on a path of self-fulfilment, joy, and personal excellence is to pursue your dreams. One life, many opportunities! Turn every opportunity into a positive new reality now rather than looking back and wishing that you had.

The heart of human excellence often begins to beat when you discover a pursuit, activity, mission, possibility, or opportunity that absorbs you, gives you freedom, challenges you, or gives you a sense of meaning, purpose, joy, or passion. Everything else can grow when you find something within a pursuit, or within yourself, that makes you feel more alive—that you are truly committed to developing.

Do you have a vision of what you would like to pursue, where you want to go, what you want to accomplish, or what you would like to do with this part of your life? If yes, then have the courage to follow your convictions. Choose to do what you want to do.

Make it clear in your mind. Think about it often. Find a way to follow the path you would like to pursue—a path with heart.
If you do not have a vision of something specific you would like to pursue, think about the direction you

might want to go, what you might like to accomplish and how you might make it happen. Even if you do not start with a big commitment to a specific goal, simply getting focused on doing good things you want to do will take you in positive directions and good things will begin to happen. Your commitment, joy, focus, and performance will grow if you are on your desired path.

Commitment is an essential ingredient guiding the pursuit of excellence. You can achieve almost anything with commitment. Conversely, high-level goals within your grasp become virtually impossible to attain if you lack commitment. Commitment to excellence requires a specific focus. Your commitment will grow when your focus is centred on:

- Continuing to learn and grow.
- Pursuing your dreams and making meaningful contributions.
- Becoming the best that you can.
- Developing your mental, physical, and technical links to excellence.
- Setting clear personal goals and relentlessly pursuing them.
- Persisting through obstacles, even when they appear insurmountable or impossible.
- Continuing to learn how to enhance the quality and consistency of your best focus and performance and acting on the lessons learned.
- Keeping the joy and passion in your pursuit.
  The roots of excellence are nurtured by engaging yourself in doing something you want and like to do.

Having a positive vision of where you want to go—in your sport, performance, relationships, or life generally inspires high levels of excellence.

You must either have or develop a passionate or life-enhancing reason for any challenging pursuit; otherwise, you will not succeed in that pursuit. You need a good reason, powerful enough to help you sustain your goals through the ups and downs of the journey.

High levels of personal commitment grow naturally out of love for what you do, combined with a positive vision of where you want to go and what you are willing to do to get there. The commitment continues to grow from embracing the special moments, absorbing yourself in your mission, overcoming obstacles, and loving the experience of ongoing personal growth.

If you enjoy what you are doing (at least parts of it) and remain focused, you will become highly competent at it—which is a worthy and beneficial goal. If you want to become great at something and continue to perform at high levels over extended periods, you usually have to love it or at least love parts of it.

Most excellent performers at the highest levels say that the pursuit itself becomes their passion and drives their lives in positive ways for extended periods. They are passionate about their pursuits, love the joyful parts, and are willing to put up with or focus through the tough parts to get to where they want to go. They draw positive energy from the parts they like and learn lessons from the parts that are not joyful.

High-level performers can achieve most of their goals and grow from their journey by focusing on something positive every day and staying committed to their goals through the negatives or obstacles. Some obstacles may initially seem insurmountable on the path to excellence.

Every performer experiences this feeling, even the greatest performers in the world. You will probably prove yourself right even when you are wrong if you believe that some obstacles are too great to overcome.

In executing with excellence, you can overcome impossible obstacles by seeing possibilities, focusing on what is within your control, taking the first step, and then focusing on the next step and the step after that.

If your commitment wavers, remember your dream goal or mission and why it is important to you. Find simple joys in your daily pursuits, rejoice in the little victories or small steps forward, and embrace the process of ongoing learning.

You will get through, focus through, or find a way through all the obstacles with a positive perspective and persistence. The commitment you make to yourself to go after your goals and persist through adversity is a huge part of reaching high-level goals. Equally important is your commitment to taking time for mental, physical, and emotional recovery.

Relaxation and regeneration are critical parts of consistent high-level performance, especially long-term.

Sometimes the best way to enhance your performance and your life is to listen to your body, listen to your heart, and respect your basic needs for relaxation, rest, personal space, good nutrition, and joyful moments away from your performance domain.

Failure to respect your needs for finding some balance between quality training and exertion and high-quality rest, between stress and relaxation, will eventually affect your performance, your life, and your love for what you are doing.

Commit to focusing on doing things that will be most beneficial to you and your ultimate goals (short-term and long-term). Respect your need for rest and recovery.

Embrace simple joys away from your training or performance sites.

Excellence requires an incredible commitment to persist through the ups and downs associated with becoming your best and maintaining your top performance. You must ignite something within that drives you to excel. You must not only commit yourself to the goal of excelling but must also commit yourself to act daily in ways that lead you to excel.

This includes committing yourself to engage in ongoing, high-quality preparation (mental, physical and technical) and committing yourself to give your best for the entire performance. It also means setting clear personal goals and relentlessly pursuing them.

To excel at the highest level, commitment moves to the point at which the pursuit itself becomes the centre of your life, at least for certain extended periods while you are engaged in preparation and performances.
The world's best performers carry an extremely high level of commitment or passion for their pursuit. This is required to attain the highest levels of excellence.

You must commit not only to high-quality training and maximum performance but also to adequate recovery to achieve consistent high-level performance. Allowing enough time for physical and mental regeneration is a critical part of high-quality performance.

You must learn to "train smart" and listen to your own body. You must respect your basic needs for relaxation, rest, rejuvenation, sleep, good nutrition and joyful moments away from your performance domain.

You are susceptible to over-training, loss of focus, inconsistent performance, chronic fatigue, irritability, illness, and injury if you fail to respect your needs for rest and regeneration. What you do away from the performance pitch has a tremendous effect on what you do in the performance arena.

One of the greatest challenges of ongoing excellence lies in respecting changing needs and ensuring that your current commitment is directed towards benefiting you and your ultimate goals.

This requires that you establish a positive personal balance between quality training/performance and quality rest/relaxation. It also means that you adjust the balance as necessary, as you move along your path of personal excellence.

The single-mindedness that permits you to attain the highest levels of excellence is not necessarily what allows you to continue to excel. Ongoing excellence requires that you respect your individual needs and create the focus that gives you the freedom to perform.

Once your technical or physical skills have become highly polished, your commitment must be balanced with trust, rest and joyful diversion to avoid overload. This will allow regeneration and enable you to return to the performance arena feeling energized, positive, confident and focused.

2. Consistency

Performing at your best consistently is one of the biggest and most difficult challenges performers in virtually all high-performance domains face. Athletes, coaches, teachers, dancers, musicians, singers, actors, surgeons, astronauts, military units, and corporate leaders all face this challenge.

The key to performing your best consistently is to respect the focus that works best for you in your training, practices, simulations, pre-performance preparation, and real-world performances.

You also need to respect your ongoing needs for rest, relaxation, recovery, adequate sleep, simple joys, healthy nutrition, and positive interaction with others to sustain high-level performance. Your best performance depends on how well you can attain and sustain your fully connected focus the moment you enter your performance arena.

You will consistently perform your best when you bring your positive and fully connected focus into every performance and sustain that focus for the duration of your game, race, mission, interaction, or performance.

Your challenge for consistency rests solidly in respecting your own best focus when you understand or discover that focus liberates you to feel and perform at your peak. This holds regardless of what your best performance might be at this point in your life— performance domain, personal interactions or career.

You need to troubleshoot properly when your performance or parts of your performance falter or fall short of your potential. Something is always responsible—you are probably at least momentarily failing to respect the focus that works best for you to bring out your true potential.

You do not lose your physical, technical, or communication skills from one moment to the next, from one day to the next, or from one week to the next.

What you lose, or what you are missing when you are not performing your best is almost always the fully connected focus that gives the freedom to perform and interact to your true capacity.

In the pursuit of excellence, you will win your quest for consistency by finding and sustaining a positive, fully connected focus that works best for you.

Over the course of your life or performance career, continue to refine and improve the focus that brings out your best performance consistently. There is always a way of focusing that brings out the best in you and your performance. There is also a way of focusing that prevents you from being your best or performing your best.

Continue to discover, respect, and fine-tune your focus. It is part of your quest for consistency in pursuing and sustaining excellence. If you consistently perform close to your potential, you have probably learned to do four things effectively:

1. Direct and connect your focus in positive and fully connected ways.
2. Channel your thoughts and emotions in positive directions.

3. Bounce back from setbacks quickly and efficiently.
4. Act on the positive lessons you are learning and apply them in your next performance situation.

Consistent high-level performers continue to respect, improve, and refine their focusing skills so they can concentrate completely on what they are engaged in to perform their best.

They avoid momentary distractions by quickly shifting focus from negative to positive, from off-target to on-target, and from disconnected to connected.

This helps them to face and overcome challenges, self-doubts, stress, errors, or setbacks they may be experiencing.

You can also do this to increase your chances of getting the most out of your preparation and getting the best out of yourself when it counts the most. You will become better in many ways, and you will perform at your best if you practice focusing and refocusing in positive and fully connected ways.

Many people react to setbacks by becoming upset with themselves, getting angry at others, or losing control emotionally. This often makes them lose their best focus—ceasing to perform well, backing off, or giving up.

The sooner you learn to react to life's obstacles, setbacks, or challenges in less negative or more positive and focused ways, the better off you will be.

An optimistic focus can lead you through things you never thought you could get through and take you places you never dreamed you could go. The good news is that you always have the potential to direct or redirect your focus in positive and life-enhancing ways, even in the face of loss, setbacks, or unjustifiable treatment.

This is true not only in your sport or performance domain but also in relationships.

A setback within a game or performance (for example, making a mistake or failing to perform your best when it counts most) can drag you down, but it can also serve as a positive reminder to focus on the next step, redirect your energy more positively and productively, and analyze errors at an appropriate time (which is usually not in the middle of a performance or argument).

After the best and less-than-best games, performances, and interactions choose to find lessons that will help to focus better for the next game, performance, or interaction. Carefully reflect on what went well and what you can improve.

You may be disappointed or frustrated with certain parts of your performance or interactions, but you can move through it quickly by extracting and acting on constructive lessons you have learned that can help you become focused and happier in the future.

Clear your mind of all negative thoughts about the past or future and focus on connecting to the remaining tasks you can control.

This is the only way to free your body and mind to perform fully in the present. Someone with a tendency to lose control, fly off the handle, or dwell on the negatives might say, "Oh, it doesn't matter that much if I do it during practice or my daily life." Ah! It does matter.

If you become accustomed to the pursuit of excellence to negative thinking, getting angry, or losing emotional control, chances are that you will carry such into your performances, competitions, and relationships. In addition, negative ways of thinking and acting take much of the joy out of the sport, relationships, work, and life.

The journey to personal and performance excellence already has enough obstacles. Hence, do not add negative thinking, anger, putting yourself down or putting others down. There are no advantages to being negative or putting yourself or others down.

Choose to stay positive, relaxed, and focused on your mission because this focus is within your control and will give you a great advantage for performing your best consistently.

It will also help you to sustain or regain a sense of flow

in your performances or interactions, particularly after experiencing a negative thought, an error, an argument, or a setback.

Think about how you would prefer to respond to challenging situations you may face in the future. Set some personal goals for improving the quality and consistency of your best focus and work towards achieving those goals.

The next time something begins to go wrong in a game, performance, routine, mission, or relationship, use that feeling or experience as a signal to immediately shift your focus back to doing what you know will enhance the rest of your performance, mission, or interaction.

For example, if you lose your best focus (even momentarily) during a performance routine, program, game, race, or mission, use it as your signal to focus on the next move and other moves, each of which is within your control.

One of the things that separate top performers, individuals and organizations, apart from everyone else is the consistency of execution.

Consistency of execution has three core elements:
- Knowing the right thing to do to drive the expected results.
- Doing those things consistently, day after day.
- Continually sharpening them by improving executions.

On the individual level, salespeople may have remarkably similar backgrounds, experiences, and capabilities. They have gone through the same training; they are using the same tools. But, there are real differences in performance.

There are differences in "make-up," and basic characteristics that drive individuals who impact performance, but one of the most basic differences is the consistency of execution.

We have all experienced moments of inspiration and brilliance. We have all seen and experienced spectacular performances at one time. A sale call perfectly executed—exceeds both organizational and customer expectations.

A deal strategy perfectly executed—aligned with the customer buying process, the customer is engaged, their issues addressed, the value created, competitive issues tackled, move it forward until we get the order.

If we have been selling for some time, we have probably been through a lot of training, read some books, and have some experiences under our belts. We know what we should be doing. We know what creates success. Often, the consistency of execution is the only difference in performance. Top performers do the right things with the right people at the right time.

Most of the top performers I interact with always have a "formula" they always stick to. They may be unable to express it, but they know what it is. They know, "I have to make many prospecting calls this week to make my numbers." The goal set by management drives them less because they have internalized their personal experiences. Thus, they automatically know what works best, and they do it every time.

Likewise, in qualifying opportunities, they know what to look for, and they know how to listen to what is said and not said. They go through the same mental checklist every time they qualify a prospect. They know what works, and do it consistently, almost reflexively, regardless of what it is—planning a call, developing a deal strategy, improving shares in their account, managing their pipeline.

By contrast, others know what works, but they do not do it regardless. Perhaps, they forget. Perhaps, they are looking for shortcuts. Perhaps, they are distracted or disorganized. Things often come together, and things work exactly as they should. I think back to Hannibal, the Colonel on the A-Team—the movie—saying, "I love it when a plan comes together."

The worst performers are more likely to be oblivious to what they have done. Better performers probably recognize it, but then they move on to the next thing, forgetting what created the success. Instead of doing what has worked in the past, they may start doing the right things, but get distracted, lose focus, or forget.

Everyone knows the sales process works. We increase

our ability to win and connect more effectively with the customer if we follow the sales process. But, we often rush or allow other things to distract us, so we start skipping steps, or making it up.

Everyone knows pre-call research and planning works. But, we were distracted by doing something else, and found out we were not prepared, yet figured we could shoot from the lip, and get by.

We need to keep focusing on consistency of execution as managers coach our people. We need to catch our people doing things right and remind them of what happens when they are doing those right things. We must sit down, go through their past wins, analyze them, look at the patterns, and then start replicating them.

Athletes do this all the time. They focus on the right things, practising over and over until it becomes "muscle memory". Whether it is perfecting a golf stroke, tennis serves, swimming stroke, hitting a baseball or passing a soccer ball. They strive to get their minds and bodies to execute consistently, almost reflexively.

Effective organizations do not necessarily have the best strategy, but they have the best and most consistent execution patterns. We see thousands of organizations have moments of brilliance.

They bring the right products to the right customers at

the right time. They develop and grow the right customers. They bring the right people on board and engage the right stakeholders. They make the right investments. But then they fade, nonetheless. They are unable to repeat or sustain the performance. It is not a strategy issue. It is the inability to execute excellent processes consistently—simultaneously firing all cylinders always.

Too often, many successful organizations do not examine what is responsible for their success. Instead, they create "strategies du jour." Trying something today, never giving it a chance, jumping onto something new tomorrow.

They never stick with something long enough to learn what works and what does not. They never recognize success patterns, replicate them and grow their experience base.

Some of the highest-performing organizations are not the first to enter the market. They do not necessarily have the most exciting products. They may not be in high-growth markets. They may be a little boring. However, they simply know what works.

You already know what works. You know what you should be doing and the right way to go about it. Are you doing them every day? Are you doing them when you encounter resistance? Consistent execution always helps you overcome obstacles.

As a manager, are you continually coaching your people, looking for that consistency that drives sustained performance? The worst thing you can do is shift priorities and change directions. Look for the patterns that drive success in everyone and the organization. Keep doing them, sharpen the execution, and maintain the momentum to "muscle memory."

The final element of consistency in execution is sharpening the saw. It is constantly trying to improve what you are doing. It is building on the base of successful experience and trying to do better—whether it is shortening a sales cycle, reducing the number of calls or improving the impact of each meeting.

From a corporate perspective, it might be improving communication and alignment, improving recruitment, or creating better customer experiences.

Everybody has the same tools, within a certain leeway but only one individual wins. It is that individual with the greatest desire and directed focus. Very small differences create very distinctive leverages towards winning.

First and foremost, you must learn to concentrate. Many things are probably going through your head, and you must see to it that these things bring you to one point and you leave the others.

"Once I start the surgery, I remain focused on each step of the surgery. As I make the skin incision, I'm focusing, concentrating on the layers below the skin. Each step has its focus." **(Elite Neurosurgeon).**

3. **Confidence and Composure**

    The third element of excellence is your BELIEF or CONFIDENCE in:

- Your potential.
- The meaningfulness of your pursuit.
- Your focus.
- Your capacity to achieve your goal(s).
- Your preparation or readiness.
- Those with whom you work or play.

Confidence and composure are positive assets that can make you feel your best, be your best, connect with your best, perform at your best, and interact more freely and positively with anyone in any context. Look for good reasons to be confident in yourself and be confident that you can live and perform to your maximum capacity.

Write down some positive reasons to be confident in yourself and in your capacity to achieve your goals and live your dreams. Read these positive reminders to yourself daily and add to them as you find additional good reasons to be confident in yourself and your mission.

To perform at your best, continue to remind yourself of the good reasons to be confident in yourself and your mission. In your performance activities, focus on executing your performance and nothing else. Nothing else matters for those moments in time.

You greatly enhance your chances of performing to your true potential when you choose to believe in yourself and your mission. Just focus on doing what you are doing and nothing else.

Everyone who spoke on the wheel of excellence can help you to strengthen your confidence. It can help you to perform consistently, closer to your potential in any context.

Your focus, commitment, mental readiness, positive imagery, confidence, distraction control, and commitment to ongoing learning and improvement all work together to free you to perform your best and live your dreams in your performance domain and all other parts of your life.

Confidence is not an event. It is grown, nurtured and allowed to blossom. All you need is to apply the processes below.

Ways to Become Confident:
- Confidence grows when you choose to see yourself as competent, committed, caring and as a skilled athlete, performer, or person capable of doing what you want to do.
- Confidence grows when you remind yourself of your best experiences, the best training, the best performances, and the best focus in your everyday pursuits, practices, performances, games, auditions,

shows, competitions, and other life-enhancing pursuits.

A positive and fully connected focus is the most important element of excellence. That is why it is the centre of the wheel of excellence.

Your focus is your core or foundation for excellence, the centre of the circle, and the hub of your wheel of excellence.

People who consistently perform their best or excel at the highest levels have learned how to focus in positive and fully connected ways. To perform at your best, you need to find and respect the focus that frees you to be the way you want to be within your performance context and in your life activities outside your performance engagements.

Excellence begins to blossom when you begin to trust yourself to completely focus on positive ways that connect with you entirely on each step in the moment-by-moment process of your performance pursuits.

A positive and fully connected focus allows you to raise the quality, level, and consistency of your best performances. The choice to raise the quality, consistency, and connectedness of your focus automatically helps you to continue to learn, experiment, grow, create, enjoy, and perform closer to your full capacity.

There is a strong link between consistency in your

performance and self-confidence. The former begins to flow naturally when you develop the latter with unwavering focus, knowing that your connected focus will get you to your destination. Consistent high-level performance depends on high-quality focus.

Develop, direct, fully connect, and sustain your best focus for the duration of your performance. This strengthens all elements of excellence that add quality and consistency to your performance and brings joy to your life.

All elements of excellence (positive and fully connected focus, commitment, mental readiness, positive images, confidence, distraction control, and ongoing learning) grow from your focus.

Your focus directs them, connecting and reconnecting you with your positive mission, making personal excellence possible.

The seven essential elements in the wheel of excellence empower you to become the person and performer you have the potential to be. All that is required of you is to act on each of these elements of excellence—all of which are within your personal control.

"The focus is so clear that you shut your thoughts off and you trust yourself and believe in yourself. You've already prepared for years and years. All you do is go, it's very natural." (**Kerrin Lee Gartner Olympic Champion – Alpine Skiing**)

Excellence is guided by a belief in your potential, your goal, the meaningfulness of your aims, and trust in your capacity to reach that goal. You must believe that you are investing in something worthwhile and that you have a good chance of making it happen before you can excel.

Believing in yourself, your teammates, and your mission enhances commitment and strengthens your overall depth of confidence and commitment.

Therefore, always reinforce your belief in the people and/or organizations with whom you work towards pursuing a collective goal. Your journey will become a lot better when you know these people value you, believe in you and are committed to your goals and development.

Individuals, teams, groups and organizations do not excel in a vacuum. They need the stimulation and support of other good people to excel. We all need at least one person who believes in us, makes us feel competent, loves us or supports our goals and dreams.

Your unwavering commitment towards a common goal births excellence within a team or group. Excellence is guaranteed when they genuinely believe they can achieve their goals, when each team member feels he or she has a meaningful role to play in pursuing that goal when they are treated with respect, and when there is a strong sense of ownership, collaboration and mutual support in pursuing the overall goal of the team. Respect and mutual support directly affect commitment and belief. Being treated with respect and challenged in positive ways enhances your commitment and your belief in your capacity to excel. Anything that strengthens belief gives you the freedom to perform at a higher level.

Believing in yourself and being confident in your ability opens you to new vistas and helps you create opportunities, pushing through all performance barriers. Doors to higher levels of excellence always open where there is an unwavering belief in your capacity to carry out a mission and an absolute connection with your performance.

Performance wavers when negative thoughts interfere with trust. In the same way, that belief can unlock doors, doubts can place limits on possibilities and potential. Your performance blossoms with belief, but the reverse is the case in the absence of belief.

The extent to which you grow to believe in yourself depends on the extent to which you live and experience concrete events that serve to enhance your belief. Thinking and acting in positive ways strengthen your self-confidence.

You can nurture the development of a strong sense of confidence in yourself by engaging in thorough high quality technical, physical, and mental preparation; experiencing success in training simulations or performances; looking for the positive parts of all performances; talking to yourself in positive ways about your experiences and capacity, and continuously drawing out constructive lessons to improve and refine the quality of your performance.

People rarely begin a sport or other high-performance pursuits with total belief in their capacity to execute tasks with precision.

You often do not know what you can do. Rookie surgeons in an operating theatre and rookie athletes in a competition arena acquire belief through experiences in the performance and practice arena from which they learn and grow.

Experiencing improvement and success, learning from others, receiving positive, constructive feedback, and feeling the support of others normally strengthen belief. Furthermore, developing essential mental skills associated with excellence also strengthens belief.

Each of these mental skills enriches the quality of preparation and the consistency of your performance in "the arena," all of which enhance belief. Strong mental skills strengthen confidence and enhance commitment. And, you often act in ways that further improve your belief and the level of your performance with increased commitment.

Belief is a two-way phenomenon. It opens the door to higher levels of excellence, and higher levels of excellence open the door to higher levels of belief. You may occasionally perform well without fully believing in yourself, but your level of trust in yourself must reach a high level to excel to your potential.

4. Control
The fourth element of excellence is CONTROLLING DISTRACTIONS to:

- Maintain an effective focus.
- Regain an effective focus after distraction, during or after a performance.
- Quickly re-enter "the zone" of high performance.
- Perform consistently at a high level.
- Stick with your game plan.
- Get adequate rest.
- Stay on your own best path for personal excellence.

The military trains in unimaginable environments. They are trained to provide medical care in the dark, while taking fire, in full body armour, after a 12-mile ruck march, with drill instructors screaming in their faces, with one arm, and any other off-the-wall scenario that could be thrown at them.

They are proficient at performing under high levels of stress and with any distraction imaginable. Their job is to remain calm, cool and collected at any time. They must remain in complete control and focused on the task at hand to achieve their goal.

You must control all distractions around you if you want to perform at your best. Distraction control is your ability to maintain or regain a positive, effective focus when faced with potential interferences, negative input, or setbacks. These distractions may be external, arising from your environment, or internal, arising from your thinking or expectations.

The important thing is not to allow people to jump around and go hysterical in the wake of a catastrophe. You just must remain calm, be in complete control and focus on your goal.

Maintaining and regaining a constructive focus is a critical part of performing to your capacity consistently—whether distractions occur before, during, in between or after events. Developing your ability to refocus in a positive direction is an extremely important factor affecting the consistency of performance in all domains.

You may experience lapses in concentration or setbacks during a performance; your goal is to quickly regain full focus. This is possible by planning to refocus and refining your ability to use cues, images, or reminders to rapidly refocus on what is within your immediate control at that moment.

Distraction control (or refocusing) is the single most important mental factor affecting the consistency of high-level performance once you have developed the ability to fully focus on your task (even for moderate periods).

5. **Constructive Evaluation**
   The fifth element of excellence is CONSTRUCTIVE EVALUATION of training and performance situations to:
- Reflect upon what you did well.
- Reflect upon what you can refine or improve.
- Draw out important lessons from each experience/performance.
- Assess the role of your commitment, attitude, and mental readiness, and focus on your performance outcome.
- Target areas for improvement.
- Act upon the lessons learned.

It has become more important to identify, as closely as possible, where you have screwed up, and then work on that in practice to make sure it does not happen again. You will sit back now after a race to analyze it with a fine-tooth comb.

I can pick a stroke here and there that may have affected the outcome of the race. When I do that and find out I missed the fifth stroke off the line, or the stroke was still short and should be long, or my transition was not as good as it should be, I can go back and work on that phase of my race and get the kinks out. Analyzing my race, stroke for stroke, and figuring out what I did wrong, can help fashion out a more perfect race.

"The idea is to try and recall exactly what happened in the race and gain from it. I'm always repeating the plan in practice and working on certain points that I can identify as screw-ups in a previous race." **(Larry Cain - Olympic Champion - Canoeing)**

"We debrief extensively. We go through every single flight, every turn. What did you do here? What cues were you using, how did you do that, and how did you make the aeroplane do that? And we try to learn from each experience. The reason we all do that in peacetime is so that we know we're as competent as anybody can be so that if we have to go fight with those things, we're better than anybody else." **(Elite Fighter Pilot)**

"You get into a sort of routine where you debrief yourself, learn from your mistakes and then when the next sim starts, it is a different ball game." **(Astronaut)**

Excellence requires that you develop an effective process for personal evaluation, and act upon the lessons drawn from these assessments. Constructive evaluation includes looking for the good things and targeting areas for personal improvement, your performance, your environment and your experiences.

You can draw inspiration, confidence and joy from reflecting on positive experiences and personal highlights.

You will gain important lessons by evaluating your overall performance, critical portions of your performance, and the role your mental state played in your performance (for example, mental readiness, trust, distraction control and sustained focus). Constructive evaluation of mental and physical performance skills requires two things:

1. Reflecting on what went well.
2. Targeting the areas for continued improvement.

Top performers have developed constructive evaluation procedures that are highly individualized and personally effective. This guides their continued pursuit of excellence.

A continuous evaluation of your preparation and focus is necessary to achieve your highest performance level. The lessons you gain can be written down, discussed, or mentally reviewed. The important point is that you develop an effective evaluation procedure to harness necessary lessons, and act accordingly.

The extent to which you engage in thorough, ongoing, constructive personal evaluation directly affects your learning rate and the performance level you ultimately attain.

Chapter 6: Excellence Quotes

The pursuit of excellence is a sine qua non for living life to the fullest, making maximum impact on those around us.

We should all strive to do our best in all areas of life. Ensure you undertake your endeavours with a spirit of excellence—whether you are building an enterprise, writing a book, hosting an event or making a presentation, do it to the best of your abilities and make it memorable.

Excellence is an indispensable quality you must possess if you want to reach your fullest potential and make the maximum impact in the world. You must prioritize excellence in all your endeavours to achieve real fulfilment and satisfaction in life. Ensure you perform beyond the set expectations on anything you are working on. If you are in business, strive to go beyond the bottom line. Be the best in all the things you embark on. I am confident the quotes in this chapter will inspire you to pursue a life of excellence.

Excellence is going beyond average and outperforming the expectations of others. It is ascending higher than the set standard. While many people settle for mediocrity, go beyond the norms. Reject the idea of only doing enough to get by.

Excellence is the accumulation of hundreds of minute decisions; it is execution at the most grandiose level. You are sliding into mediocrity once you accept the idea that you should give in to things that make no sense because other people do those things, and you want to appear reasonable.

Although it is easy to go along with what everyone else is doing, try to be extraordinary and function with excellence. Strive to make a difference and rise above average practices. To help you reach your highest potential, below is a collection of inspirational, wise, and powerful excellence quotes, obtained from a variety of sources over the years. Enjoy!

The pursuit of excellence with unrestrained passion can lead to the accomplishment of wonders with unsurpassed joy – **Aberjhani**

Persistence is the twin sister of excellence. One is a matter of quality; the other is a matter of time— **Habeeb Akande**

Seeking excellence means choosing to forge your sword to cut through the limitations of your life— **James A. Murphy**

Either find a way or make one You can bend but you can never break if you want to achieve excellence —**Ziad K. Abdelnour**

Excellence is in the details. Give attention to the details in everything you do and excellence will come—**Perry Sexton**

If you want to achieve excellence, you must refuse to let anything stand in the way of your potential —**Sai Pradeep**

You can shine and make a mark in some field. Your job is to find your niche, excel and build a lasting legacy—**Roopleen**

Do you know great minds enjoy excellence, average minds love mediocrity and small minds adore comfort zones? —**Onyi Anyado**

Be driven with purpose. Be relentless in your alignment with excellence. Pay no mind to the disimpassioned impotent haters —**Steve Maraboli**

When you uncommonly do the common things, you'll command the attention of the world—**George Washington Carver**

Step out of the crowd of average people. Enter that game and change the values on the scoreboard—**Israelmore Ayivor**

Our attitude to focus on excellence not only made us successful but also timelessly inspirational —**Kishore Bansal**

If you don't value excellence, you won't achieve excellence —**Glenn C. Stewart**

The future belongs to only those who would attain excellence in the field of their own choice—**Abhijit Naskar**

The excellent person manages himself. He will not allow the environment to manage him —**Rex Resurreccion**

Do ordinary things extraordinarily well —**Gregg Harris**

A passive mindset "manages" to live with mediocre, but an active mindset "leads" to change until excellence results —**Orrin Woodward**

The person who will end up enjoying success is the one who planned for it and who knew why they are seeking to succeed—**Archibald Marwizi**

Moderation leads to Mediocrity; Intensity leads to Excellence —**Suleman Abdullah**

Virtue is excellence, something uncommonly great and beautiful, which rises far above what is vulgar and ordinary —**Adam Smith**

I don't settle in any other area of my life when it comes to excellence, so why should I lower my standards when it comes to boys —**Adriana Trigiani**

Happiness is the full use of one's talents along lines of excellence—**John F. Kennedy**

If you are going to achieve excellence in big things, you develop the habit in little matters. Excellence is not an exception; it is a prevailing attitude —**Charles R. Swindoll**

Excellence prospers in the absence of excuses—**Lorii Myers**
The quality of people's lives is in direct proportion to their commitment to excellence, regardless of their chosen field of endeavour—**Vincent Lombardi**

Blossoming out through one's comfort zone should be well-meaning so as to achieve newer levels of excellence." —**Priyavrat Thareja**

The   race   for   excellence   has   no   finish line—**Mohammed bin Rashid Al Maktoum**

I hope you will simply do what you can do in the best way you know. If you do so, you will witness miracles come to pass—**Gordon B. Hinckley**

There are no shortcuts to excellence —**Angela Duckworth**

A visionary is a leader of excellence who sees what others do not see, who achieves for now and plans for the future, who positively impacts different generations and raises other visionaries—**Onyi Anyado**

Excellence quotes that will inspire you to do your best.

Excellence is a direct result of extra effort. —**Gift Gugu Mona.**

Your customers will always be people. Empathy and a smile are your revenue builder. —**Janna Cachola.**

If the 'Journey of 1000 miles begins with a single step' – that is prescribed to – ALIGN. —**Priyavrat Thareja.**

The less justified a man is in claiming excellence for his self, the more ready is he to claim all excellence for his nation, his religion, his race or his holy cause. —**Eric Hoffer**

Perfect may not always be pretty but excellence is always elegant. —**Janna Cachola**

A timely benefit, -though a thing of little worth, the gift itself, -in excellence transcends the earth. —**Thiruvalluvar**

People simply feel better about themselves when they're good at something. —**Stephen R. Covey**

People of excellence go the extra mile to do what's right. —**Joel Osteen**

Don't let the fact you haven't done something before convincing you that you can't do it, or that it cannot be done perfectly the first time you try your hand at it. —**A.J. Darkholme**

It's better to do one thing well than ten things poorly. —**Heather Hart**

We can never achieve and succeed without first making excellence second nature. —**Jolene Church**

Always give your best; today's great work is tomorrow's benchmark. —**Ifeanyi Enoch Onuoha**

Don't wait for a huge platform before you give your best performance. —**Bernard Kelvin Clive**

What is good is difficult, and what is difficult is rare.

—Robert Farrar Capon

Time only gives one chance, if you lose it once, you can never get it back. **—Sunday Adelaja**

Excellence is the result of caring more than others think is wise, risking more than others think is safe, dreaming more than others think is practical, and expecting more than others think is possible. **—Ronnie Oldham**

Be a character of excellence, not excuses. **—Janna Cachola**

Excellence must be achieved through the eyes of those who judge us; once achieved it can only be maintained with constant innovation. **—Tom Collins**

Bring your dreams to reality. Believe in yourself. You know you have what it takes to make your dreams come true. Start now and dedicate yourself to success. Shoot for the stars and make it happen. **—Mark F. LaMoure**

Excellence is never an accident. It is always the result of high intention, sincere effort, and intelligent execution; it represents the wise choice of many alternatives - choice, not chance, determines your destiny. **—Aristotle**

Excellence is the gradual result of always striving to do better. **—Pat Riley**

If you want to achieve excellence, you can get there today. As of this second, quit doing less-than-excellent work. —**Thomas J. Watson**

Excellence is not a skill. It is an attitude. —**Ralph Marston**

If you cannot do great things, do small things in a great way. —**Napoleon Hill**

If you are going to achieve excellence in big things, you develop the habit in little matters. Excellence is not an exception; it is a prevailing attitude. —**Colin Powell**

Excellence is doing ordinary things extraordinarily well. —**John W. Gardner**

The road to excellence is always under construction. —**unknown**

Superiority -- doing things a little better than anybody else can do them. —**Orison Swett Marden**

It is quality rather than quantity that matters. —**Seneca**

Excellence is rarely found, more rarely valued. —**Johann Wolfgang**

Doing common things uncommonly well. —**Orison Swett Marden**

About excellence, it is not enough to know, but we must try to have and use it. —**Aristotle**

Excellence encourages one about life generally; it shows the spiritual wealth of the world. —**George Eliot**

We are what we repeatedly do. Excellence, then, is not an act, but a habit. —**Aristotle**

Supreme excellence consists in breaking the enemy's resistance without fighting. —**Sun Tzu**

Next to excellence is the appreciation of it. —**William Makepeace Thackeray**

The sad truth is that excellence makes people nervous. —**Shana Alexander**

Excellence is the unlimited ability to improve the quality of what you have to offer—**Rick Pitino**

Excellence is about fighting and pursuing something diligently, with a strict and determined approach to doing it right. It's okay if there are flaws in the process - it makes it more interesting. —**Charlie Trotter**

There is no real excellence in all of this world which can be separated from the right living. —**David Starr Jordan**

Excellence always sells. —**Earl Nightingale**

Excellence means when a man or woman asks of himself more than others do. —**Jose Ortega Y Gasset**

Those who attain any excellence, commonly spend life in one pursuit; for excellence is not often gained upon easier terms. —**Samuel Johnson**

The pursuit of excellence is less profitable than the pursuit of bigness, but it can be more satisfying. —**David Ogilvy**

All human excellence is but comparative. There may be persons who excel us, as much as we fancy, we excel the meanest. —**Samuel Richardson**

Excellence is a process that should occupy all our days. —**Theodore Wilhelm Engstrom**

He who does it first may do well, but he who does it best will do better. —**Scott Allen**

The desire of excellence is the necessary attribute of those who excel. We work little for a thing unless we wish for it. —**Edward G. Bulwer-Lytton**

Excellence is an art won by training and habituation. We do not act rightly because we have virtue or excellence, but we rather have those because we have acted rightly. —**Will Durant**

Quality in a service or product is not what you put into it. It is what the client or customer gets out of it. **—Peter Drucker**

Customers don't expect you to be perfect. They do expect you to fix things when they go wrong. **—Don Porter**

The single most important thing to remember about any enterprise is that there are no results inside its walls. The result of a business is a satisfied customer. **—Peter Drucker**

Excellence is an art won by training and habituation. We do not act rightly because we have virtue or excellence, but we rather have those because we have acted rightly. We are what we repeatedly do. Excellence, then, is not an act but a habit. **—Aristotle**

Nothing great was ever achieved without enthusiasm. **—Ralph Waldo Emerson**

There are no traffic jams along the extra mile. **—Roger Staubach**

Do what you do so well that they will want to see it again and bring their friends. **—Walt Disney**

If a man is called to be a street sweeper, he should sweep streets even as Michelangelo painted, or Beethoven composed music or Shakespeare wrote poetry. He should sweep streets so well that all the hosts of heaven and earth will pause to say, 'Here lived a great street sweeper who did his job well. —**Martin Luther King Jr.**

My meaning simply is, that whatever I have tried to do in life, I have tried with all my heart to do well; that whatever I have devoted myself to, I have devoted myself to completely; that in great aims and in small, I have always been thoroughly in earnest. —**Charles Dickens**

Mediocrity will never do. You are capable of something better. —**Gordon B. Hinckley**

We should not judge people by their peak of excellence, but by the distance, they have travelled from the point where they started. —**Henry Ward Beecher**

If I cannot do great things, I can do small things in a great way. —**Martin Luther King Jr.**

Anything worth doing is worth doing right—**Hunter S Thompson**

If you don't have time to do it right, when will you have the time to do it over? —**John Wooden**
Focus on making yourself better, not on thinking that you are better. —**Bohdi Sanders**
Do your best, and be a little better than you are—**Gordon B. Hinckley**

To be successful you have to be selfish, or else you

never achieve. And once you get to your highest level, then you have to be unselfish. Stay reachable. Stay in touch. Don't isolate. —**Michael Jordan**

We all want to be extraordinary and we all just want to fit in. Unfortunately, extraordinary people rarely fit in. —**Sebastyne Young**

I do the very best I know how, the very best I can, and I mean to keep on doing so until the end. —**Abraham Lincoln**

People of excellence go the extra mile to do what's right. —**Joel Osteen**

Excellence is an art won by training and habituation. We do not act rightly because we have virtue or excellence, but we rather have those because we have acted rightly. We are what we repeatedly do. Excellence, then, is not an act but a habit. —**Aristotle**

Some people insist that 'mediocre' is better than 'best.' They delight in clipping wings because they themselves can't fly. They despise brains because they have none. —**Robert A. Heinlein**

If you don't have time to do it right, when will you have time to do it again? —**John Wooden**

To seek greatness is the only righteous vengeance. —**Criss Jami**

As Aristotle said, 'Excellence is a habit.' I would say furthermore that excellence is made constant through the feeling that comes right after one has completed a work, which he himself finds undeniably awe-inspiring. He only wants to relax until he's ready to renew such a feeling all over again because to him, all else has become absolutely trivial. **—Criss Jami**

Excellence is to do a common thing in an uncommon way. **—Booker T. Washington**

Perfection is not attainable, but if we chase perfection, we can catch excellence. **—Vince Lombardi**

In the land where excellence is commended, not envied, where weakness is aided, not mocked, there is no question as to how its inhabitants are all superhuman. **— Criss Jami**

We don't get a chance to do that many things, and everyone should be excellent. Because this is our life. **—Steve Jobs**

YOUR ORGANIZATION

Chapter 7: Building an Organizational Culture of Excellence.

Your corporate culture would be the operating system if your business were a computer. You must have the right operating system in place; otherwise, your software programs simply will not work. Ditto your business.

The absence of the right corporate culture will prevent you from achieving your performance goals—no matter how much time and money you spend.

Many executives mistakenly conceptualize corporate culture as an intangible concept. So, when their companies experience challenges, they turn to what they consider to be more concrete solutions like team building or skills training. Unfortunately, these activities are akin to putting out little bushfires without considering the current climate or environment. They tend to address only the symptoms and not the core problem.

In reality, corporate culture is a tangible concept that can be quantified and measured. By working on your corporate culture, you are addressing the core cause of any problems you may be experiencing and accessing the solution to real growth and the business results you want to achieve.

Some companies mistakenly limit their corporate culture development to just their leadership or executive team hoping that it will simply trickle down to the rest of the organization. Or, they may think they have a revenue problem or a customer service problem and limit their focus to specific teams.

While there are times that high-performance companies experience particular issues related to a single team, the most successful companies focus on building a wide organizational culture of excellence. They understand that every part of the organization has an impact on the other parts and that the most powerful results are created when every part is in sync.

By focusing on every employee and team across the organization, you will ensure that each individual:
- Aligns to an inspiring and meaningful shared vision towards which the entire organization works.

- Understands the end goal, the company's status quo and, specifically, how to bridge the gap between the two.

Seven Ways You Can Build an Organizational Culture of Excellence

Leadership Excellence: No amount of leadership development and skills training will ever make a difference if the executives and managers do not have the right mindset in place. Distractions due to feelings of powerlessness, insecurity, avoidance, resentment, fear of change, or a protectionist mentality will prevent them from being fully open, and interested in the new learning.

However, if you focus on building the appropriate leadership culture and mindset first, fears, resentment and confidence issues will be transformed into opportunities for growth, greater team cohesion and collaboration and a leadership team that is engaged and ready to learn.

Team members feel encouraged and supported by leaders who have the right outlook and truly apply practical leadership and coaching skills. Of course, team members know that their roles and work matter, and it results in higher levels of motivation and independence to work towards their goals.

This helps leaders and managers to move away from nonessential tasks and babysitting and focus instead on what they are supposed to do—be strategic and improve team performance.

Leadership does not just happen. But when it is done right, the result is highly committed and engaged teams, with high levels of communication, workflow and productivity.

Sales Excellence: While it is common knowledge that a high-performance sales team is vital to the financial success of any organization, many companies simply go from one sales training program to another, getting the same results each time—short-term rises in performance and productivity that quickly drop off as salespeople drift back to their old habits and routines.

Once again, no amount of skills training can make a difference if your salespeople lack the right mindset. Your sales team may lack assertiveness, commitment or focus but if you first concentrate on building the right sales culture and mindset, fears of rejection and confidence problems go away.

Your sales team will be more confident, assertive, receptive and accountable—and will be able to deal with the different challenges facing them. Teams that have achieved sales excellence operate from a customer mindset. They understand the needs and motivations of customers and partner with them to create a result that is mutually beneficial to both parties. It is all about relationships and partnership.

Customer Service Excellence: The essence of customer service excellence is the ability to create a memorable and positive experience. This experience must be unique to your organization and consistent at every level, whether it is on the phone with a representative, in person at the front desk, or speaking with the accounting department. To deliver this level of customer service, a mindset or culture of excellence is required.

Only then will your customer service teams understand that a great service experience is not created by simply applying some skills but comes from the energy and core of each person. Service excellence is the ability to create a connection with the customer so that they feel you genuinely care about the fulfilment of their needs. This generates a superior service experience that causes them to come back for more. It creates the buzz and reference base that every company wants.

Team Excellence: Most employees focus more on protecting personal agendas rather than working collaboratively with others in a spirit of openness and common interest if companies do not have that unifying element that comes from a strong corporate and team culture.

To create team excellence, there has to be a common unifying goal and aspiration that brings people together, where everyone on the team understands that by working together as a team, everyone will benefit more: individually, as a team, as an organization, and with customers.

To truly achieve team excellence, everyone must

believe that by working together, they will achieve more than by protecting their knowledge, skills and expertise.

Operational Excellence: Every team member must cultivate the right mindset and understand the specific goals they are working towards to achieve operational excellence. These goals must be motivating, and inspiring, and can only be achieved by working together.

With the right outlook, skills and coaching in place, operational teams work in the same ways that the very top sports teams operate. They are not focused on beating the other team, but rather on beating the clock, breaking records, and achieving something that has not been accomplished before. This creates excitement, energy and positive tension.

Product/Service Excellence: Product or service quality can make or mar businesses. The level of input on details, processes and quality control has a significant role in determining your place in emerging markets. Poor quality of service can result in low patronage and loss of customers.
It is important to always market quality assurance while promoting your product or services. This level of excellence brings a pool of clients and goodwill to your business or organization.

Network or Affiliation Excellence
The quality of your association reveals the quality of

your mindset. It projects your values and unearths your buried ideologies. Network and industry-based affiliations sometimes serve as excellence hotspots where credibility abounds. If I need professional advice on brain trauma, a doctor who is a member of The Canadian Neurosurgical Society would readily tick the boxes more than any other neurosurgeon. You have to know that credible affiliations enhance excellent practice.

Look around you and sign-up with sector-based networks that support and promote your business. Global trends, new research or interests are also shared amongst networks and their members. You will miss out on quality and evidence-based information if you are not a member of a professional body that regulates your industry.

Chapter 8: Excellence in Leadership

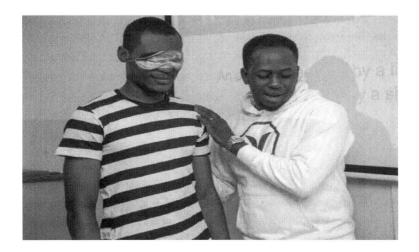

Today's business world and the workplace can be a rat race for survival amidst varying contending interests. These often impede leadership excellence.

Due to the ever-competitive nature of doing business today, most companies are beginning to realize that to stay on top of their game in the industry, they need players and employees who have what it takes to lead the company to business success and more. Greater emphasis is now being placed on a workforce built on excellent leadership qualities that guarantee optimum performance and productivity.

Below are twelve ways to ensure you become an effective leader who brings excellent leadership to your work and inspires all-around productivity and effective team spirit.

1. **Be Original**

   Always be yourself—be original. And do not stop there. Ensure you are always thinking of new ways to solve problems. Think outside of the box to discover how you can help and lead the team better. You must be 10 times ahead of those you are leading.

   Not all of your ideas will be appreciated, and not all of them would work. The good news, however, is that your originality will be welcomed by those who are in search of and appreciate excellence.

   Be passionate about your idea and show how it can work to move the company forward. Remember that many business successes of our time, and in years past, are borne out of original ideas. This is the hallmark of excellent leadership. If you are not passionate about your idea and why you believe it would work, no one will believe in it either.

2. **Support a Struggling Colleague**

   Always be willing to lend a helping hand to an ailing colleague. Remember that it is all about the collective efforts brought to the table. Effective leaders know this. When a part or fraction of the chain is weak, the entire chain becomes as weak. As the saying goes, *you are only as strong as your weakest link.*

   Empathize with your struggling colleagues. When you

can, support them physically and emotionally, ensuring the work is excellently done no matter what. Such altruism will endear you to your colleagues and employers and make you stand out as a leader who can inspire his team to greatness because he works with them side by side, helping when things are challenging and being there whenever the need arises.

3. **Be an Effective Team Player**
   The ability to work in a team and for the team is another hallmark of an excellent business leader. Increasing ethnic, social and religious diversity in work teams today often makes it difficult for team members to readily get along due to individual differences. These differences have a way of spilling into team dynamics and can easily bring about fractures, factions and friction.

   This is where having adequate emotional intelligence comes in. Your ability to understand, manage, regulate and adapt to the different contending emotions and orientations, as well as your own emotions, will ensure you relate and connect with team members in the best way possible. This enables genuine cooperation, understanding and commitment to team ethics.

4. **Be Result-Oriented in all Your Task**
   Great business leaders know that getting results is what matters in business. They do not just get the results, they breathe and live results. And, they do this with so much pride and enthusiasm that it becomes a natural part of their personality. They approach every task with

the mindset of achieving something remarkable. They always fix their eyes on the "ball" and in the end, their energy and positivism filter through to those they lead till they achieve excellence.

You must only think of what works and how to get the needed results to become such an excellent leader. You must always target a positive outcome. This mentality inherently permeates your team members and colleagues. Consequently, it inspires everyone to go for the target.

Your enthusiasm fuels optimism. You must refuse to take failure as a conclusion. You have to strive continuously till you get results—till you obtain the outcome you seek. In turn, it boosts the belief and confidence of the team in your leadership to achieve even the impossible.

5. **Avoid the Curse of Envy**
   This is one of the foundations of all failed work teams. The scourge of jealousy and envy can bring down even the greatest of business teams. Envy and jealousy breed hate and loathing.
   This can pose damaging consequences to the underlying dynamics of the members of the company as the ill blood and negativity it generates often lead to sabotage, betrayal and the loss of trust. With these three horrible arrowheads, it becomes difficult to build unity, loyalty and a sense of community.

Therefore, you need to ensure you strive as much as

you can to reduce the degree of envy by allowing more "We" than "I" to be attached to you and your accomplishments. Learn to deflect excessive praise and acknowledge the contributions of others in whatever you achieve. Ignore self-aggrandizement. That way you would be giving your colleagues part of the credit.

This will work towards reducing the "Pull Him Down" (PhD) syndrome, as your colleagues would feel part of the successes achieved as well. Smart leaders understand this and use such leadership styles to get more out of the people while excelling in their leadership.

6. **Learn to Appreciate your Colleagues' Supportive Efforts**
A tree does not make a forest; thus, the saying goes. You cannot deny the veracity of this paradigm.

One man does not make an army. Essentially, you cannot do it all alone. You need help all the time no matter how old, informed, talented, intelligent and experienced you are. So, do not forget to thank and appreciate your colleagues when they help you with a task.

Being an excellent leader entails knowing how to get the people on your side by showing them gratitude when it is due. If someone helped you on a project, acknowledge his or her contributions.

When a colleague learns that you have put in a good

word for them for the part, they played in helping you on a project; they will be motivated to do more. Your colleagues will in turn appreciate your gratitude for appreciating their kindness. Ultimately, you would have built and guaranteed a steady flow of support when you need it. This is one of the keys to excellent leadership.

7. **Think Out of the Box, especially with Difficult Objectives**
   There is no substitute for creativity and independent thinking. All great leaders in business and politics know this.

   Creativity involves thinking outside the box to come up with innovative solutions in the pursuit of organizational objectives. Put your excellent leadership qualities to work by seeking novel ways to achieve the desired result when the set objective proves daunting.

   Do not be afraid of failing or being called names or ridiculed for your ideas. Fortune favours only the bold. Diversify your thinking and be open to the flux of ideas that rush in. Conventional methods do not always have the answers. Practice a little unorthodox thinking from time to time.

   Great answers are usually found where and when you least expect them. And, when the answers leap out at you, do not discredit them (or let anyone else) until you've had the chance to test their workability.

Your knack for innovative solutions to problems will set you out as a great mind and a go-to guy. This will stand you in great stead in the organization and solidify your leadership potential and capability.

8. **Do not Fear Failing, it is a Trap**
Fear of failure is one of the limiting factors of excellent leadership. The fear of failing often brings about an unwillingness to act and engage.

This causes stagnation and inertia. Most companies are so afraid to fail that they begin to be less adventurous. This potentially holds great ideas back from being executed.

Therefore, you must show your leadership qualities by not fearing failure's shame, rather you need to up your game to bring your organization to fame. Be convinced of your idea and believe in yourself.

Approach every task given to you with courage and belief, no matter the level of difficulty or the obstacles before you. Work hard at it until you succeed. Even when failure is a possibility, it should not be an option for you nor form your reality.

9. **Have your Eye Trained to always Focus on the Objective**
It is easy to start a project but staying on course till the end is often a big issue altogether. Many times, a company sets out to accomplish a project. Then the stakeholder simply loses interest or motivation in the

continuation of such a project and suspends it subsequently after a lot has gone in. This can harm you or any business that allows such an approach to taking root. Following through on a project takes discipline and dedication to the realization of the project.

You must, therefore, ensure that you complete all projects under your watch. Having the bigger picture in mind also helps you to maintain focus. As a leader or member of a team in the company, show your leadership qualities by working to see that objectives and targets are always achieved.

Maintain 100% focus on every task at hand. Allow less distraction and more purposeful actions. When the objective is realized, you would have presented yourself excellently and your leadership qualities shone through for all to see.

10. **Always Strive for a WIN-WIN Situation with Colleagues and Clients/Customers**
To excel in leadership, especially in the workplace, always seek **WIN-WIN** situations with both your colleagues and customers alike. Remember it is not about you; it is about the collective energies. When everyone is happy, everybody is happy.

A **WIN-WIN** situation boosts relationships both within and outside the company. You can maintain good business relationships between customers and the company by building strong relations with customers.

This guarantees continual business, which leads to improved revenue generation and profit. By building strong relations with your colleagues, you ensure that cooperation and harmony are the order of the day. A harmonious work environment is good for creativity and productivity, which also impacts the organization and business positively as well.

11. **Be Proactive**

Excellent business leadership entails a proactive culture of decision-making and engagement with customers as well as colleagues at the workplace. Leading with excellence requires anticipating things before they happen and putting the necessary steps in place to ensure a positive outcome.

Always ask yourself, "What does the team need?" "What can be done to improve the efficiency and effectiveness of how things are done?" Anticipate changes in the market before it happens and make your observation known to the owner and those in the position to take note and act on the information. And, if the responsibility falls in your lap, then get up and do something about it.

Be known for your **vision** and **proactivity**. Look out for the bigger picture and foresee events before they happen by carefully observing the numbers and keeping a keen eye on things—both within the company and outside the company, even among your competition.

Remember: no great business leadership was ever great without this quality.

It was Steve Jobs' excellent visionary and proactive business leadership, and his ability to see into the future and its astonishing numbers and go ahead to do what needs to be done to get there, even when critics criticized that same vision that has made Apple Inc. the top global brand it is today.

12. **Always Prepare for Change**

It is apt that this point follows right on the heels of **vision** and **proactivity**. Sometimes, we fail to see the picture and end up running into obstacles and challenges because we are least prepared for them.

Market forces also throw up sudden surprises that jolt businesses from their very foundations. The 2008 economic crisis that rocked the whole world is one such example of how the market can suddenly somersault and turn on its head in a sharp nose-dive (from which many businesses cannot recover).

Therefore, this is an opportunity for you to show your business leadership qualities by leading your company to develop best practices that adapt to the changes in the market at present and uncover and adopt new ways to reposition your business and the economy to weather the storm and create services and products that help the company make a profit, at the same time reduce many of the rising cost of doing business today.

Adequate preparations by naturally training yourself to

always prepare for and adapt to change, when necessary, births your competence in handling the challenges posed by market forces. This will also stand you out and place you in the Hall of Excellence.

Now, you know the ways and what you need to do to become an excellent business leader. It is interesting to note here that we need great businesses and great business leaders to build a great world.

Great businesses birth super economies. In the end, it is a **WIN-WIN** situation for the business owners, the active workers and those seeking active employment, their families, the economy and the world at large. So, become an excellent business leader today. The world needs you!

Chapter 9: Becoming a High-Performance Organization

As a leader, you do not head to work every day intending to achieve mediocre results. Nonetheless, your actions or focus may inadvertently engender mediocre expectations. Unfortunately, this is a trap that snags many organizational and business leaders.

Executive and business owners desire immediate results, accelerated performance and lasting change. However, the corporate cultures in many organizations and training programs produce only short-term gains that fade away as teams go back to their old habits.

The key to moving your organization from mediocre to a state of excellence requires a fundamental shift in your corporate culture. When you build a corporate culture of excellence, you create organizational capacity and a structure that empowers, focuses on and engages employees.

You stop wasting a tremendous amount of time and money nurturing an outmoded culture focused on problem-solving. Instead, you equip your teams with the right mindset and skills necessary to focus on creating the desired results.

A dysfunctional corporate culture can disgust your best talent and drive them away. An exciting, supportive, and empowering one can attract and retain them. As an organization, you also need to help employees develop the flexibility and resilience to deal with change, challenge and uncertainty that may arise along the way.

Keys to Becoming a High-Performance Organization

1. **Unequivocal, Compelling Organizational Vision**
   It is not enough to simply have a stated organizational vision. To become a high-performance organization, every employee must understand not only the company's vision, but also know their roles, responsibilities and the specific actions they need to take to help achieve this vision.

2. **Clear Purpose and Meaning**
   In a high-performance organization, employees feel that what they are working on is meaningful,

significant, and purpose based. Everyone concerned is highly inspired by the common purpose which becomes the driving force behind everything that they do.

3. **Mastery of Roles and Focus on High Performers**

   Most companies unconsciously apply problem-solving, and firefighting strategies and unintentionally end up rewarding mediocrity.

   Many managers enable their low performers by focusing their time and energy on trying to solve their problems while spending a disproportionately meagre amount of time on their high performers.
   Those high performers eventually leave the organization because they are not being recognized or rewarded for their hard work.

   In a high-performance organization, employees are supported and encouraged to become masters in their respective roles and areas of expertise. High performers are nurtured, rewarded, mentored and recognized, and average performers are coached to move into the high-performance category.

   In these cultures, there is no place for low performers, and they either move up or leave the organization.

   In a high-performance organization, employees develop the flexibility and resilience to deal with change, challenge and uncertainty. Even when some obstacles and challenges may seem impossible to overcome, the motivation to achieve the organizational vision is higher than the urge to avoid discomfort and pain. With that clarity of purpose and a strong desire to succeed, they push through the barriers and move forward towards their vision.

In a high-performance organization, managers support their teams in staying focused and on track, despite difficulties and challenges.

4. Highly Collaborative Teams

Most of us have worked in companies where the solo mentality reigns. Teams and individuals closely guard their expertise, projects and knowledge. Collaboration across teams is nearly non-existent unless forced.

Highly collaborative teams both internal and external are a key feature of a high-performance organization. As every employee and all teams work together towards a common organizational vision, they feel they are on the same side and collaborate effectively. And, because this cooperation is encouraged and rewarded from the top down, there is no more reason to protect individual roles, projects or expertise.

5. Pioneer Mentality

Most companies operating as high-performance organizations do not settle for mediocrity. Instead, they are focused on creating something that has never been created before—breaking records and achieving unprecedented results. From the outside, it may seem as if they are achieving the impossible.

The resulting energy, excitement and drive create a certain positive tension that reverberates throughout the company. Employees and teams are encouraged to explore, nurture and co-create to achieve common goals.

Finally, organizations need to embrace practical coaching for excellence skills to sustain their momentum long term.

Without this internal leadership and coaching capacity in place, organizations will resort to the old pattern of finding short-term solutions that fall by the wayside as employees slip back to their old habits.

By implementing that, start building a new culture of excellence and creating an organization where your employees feel empowered, inspired and motivated.

6. Adherence to Best Practices

It is very difficult to disregard best practices in your industry and be a high-performing organization at the same time. Every year, new trends and development in various sectors of industries around the world are available for adoption and execution.

This is supported by evidence-based practice in these sectors. High-performance organizations cannot afford to downplay these trends as they can result in descendant or ascendant trajectory outcomes for your organization. This supports quality improvement and brings quality assurance to your numerous clients, investors and partners.

7. Conducive Work Environment

Innovation can be buried in workspaces that are not comfortable. Yes, Apple Inc. and a few other Fortune 500 companies started in a garage, yet they didn't stay there! They evolved. Today, Facebook and Google are one of the world's most conducive spaces for developing timeless products and services.

They have **"Thinking Spaces"** where staff can hang around to trap and brood ideas that flow through their minds. For every software update that pops up on your cell phone, someone with **unrestricted mental interrogation** processes new cellular features in a supportive **environment** that makes your device-using experience memorable. (Note the words highlighted in bold letters.)

These ideas are not birthed in war zones or environments smeared with chaos. They come from conducive environments where the mind is free to wander and explore imaginative processes towards enriching the services with which you enjoy.

You need doses of inspiration to achieve excellent products or services whether you are a front desk officer, manager, production line staff or CEO. Environments can stifle or strengthen individual and corporate efforts in this direction. It comes with a price because resources have to be sunk in towards creating workspaces that trigger innovation and creativity.

Culturally appropriate language can be used to stimulate workflow within your organization. Phrases that promote a culture of creativity and exploration can serve as enduring routes to creating conducive work environments.

This will also take a collaborative effort between you and your employee, as everyone has to feel the pulse of the freedom to be original in executing various tasks. Now, back to the highlighted words.

8. Unrestricted Mental Interrogation

This cannot happen in fixed mindset environments. High-performance organizations are hubs for a growth mindset and futuristic thinking where employers are trained and allowed to apply the training.

Typical self-serving leaders do not raise leaders; they raise slaves who gulp every line, hook and sinker. This automatically limits their ability to question things, interrogate processes and problem-solve their way out of challenges.

High-performance organizations provide platforms and workspaces where deep thinkers are born, honed and deployed. My question to you is: "What is the physical and emotional appearance of your workspace? Is it inviting, unattractive or painted with denigration?" Your answer to this question will determine whether you are running a high-performance organization.

9. Supporting Environment

Boundless thinking is an upshot of supporting environments. You cannot separate the two. Timeless services and products that meet diverse population needs in the face of change are consequences of carefully altered environments that stimulate individual and group exploration.

The difference between a Kentucky Fried Chicken (KFC) outlet down the road and a burger booth is the ambience that elicits memorable consumption. They necessarily do not sell burgers and fillings, but memories. Their environment enables them to penetrate their markets, leaving customers with a "Go back" kind of feeling.

Supportive environments are idea centres that provide the needed motivation for exceptional and excellent service delivery. As you lead or prepare to start an organization or run a business, remember that environments are productivity conduits.

Your office size does not matter. Feelings that filter through those spaces are of primary importance than the beautiful piece of furniture or artwork that adorn your space.
I believe personal values such as order, attention to detail, aesthetics and appreciation of ambience are traits that you can cultivate as a leader.

These traits are primarily internal (intrinsic) and then become visibly appealing externally (extrinsic) once put into good use—a significant process to becoming a high-performance organization in your industry. Starting from the confines of your bedroom to the walls of your office, people should smell excellence a mile away.

Never downplay the role supporting environments play in building a high-performance organization. Your clients will never recover from it; your employees are the first beneficiaries. Your products or services will have a monumental effect on the lives of the people you serve. Always remember, environments matter!

Chapter 10: Business Ethics & Excellence

It is very disheartening to see businesses with amazing products and services lose worrisome tons of credibility a few years down the line. I mentioned in a previous chapter of this book that you can have a wonderful vision ruined with bad methods. Bad business conduct is one of those deficiencies that set your organization on a downward spiral by affecting your business, kith and kin, etcetera.

I have been engaged to mediate for organizations whose business practices were all shades of wrong. I respectfully declined because meddling in situations like this can leave a permanent smear on your identity and that of your corporation. A single act of individual or corporate misconduct can damage your brand in unimaginable ways.

What is Business Ethics?

The Stanford Encyclopedia of Philosophy describes business ethics as the study of the ethical dimensions of productive organizations and commercial activities. This covers ethical analyses of the production, distribution, marketing, sale and consumption of goods and services.

Looking deep into this description, we can see one of the key phrases I have treated in this book jump at us! The phrase: **"productive organizations."**

Business ethics and productivity coexist. One cannot exist without the other. Every act of business misconduct smears corporate image and productivity down the line.

Starting from product procurement to production, promotion, packaging and sales, you cannot afford to engage in shady deals that rob your organization's credibility. Some businesses tread the path of dishonour, lobbying for policies with governments that violate sustained business principles like integrity, value for human life and harm against the environment.
Some business contracts may be mouth-watering and financially rewarding, but they constitute many of the corporate flaws that cause mishaps for many organizations.

Change of government, forensic audits and aggressive advocacy efforts from Civil Society Organizations (CSOs) or Non-Governmental Organizations (NGOs) can upset the shady deals an organization engages in.

When this happens, the growth process becomes stunted and smears up all the years of effort sunk into the business. You lose credibility, stand the risk of a jail term, your business gets wound up and you leave many families with bouts of desperation on where they get the next meal.

Ethical business practices have positive long-term implications for your organization. It also serves as an organic growth promotion strategy for your business. Non-ethical business conduct, on the other hand, limits all opportunities for excellence and cripples the morals of your employees.

Business ethics and excellence are marketable aspects of corporate growth. An incredible number of organizations have become global brands through their business ethics processes. I will mention just a few of them here.

A. The Dr Pepper Snapple Group

This company has marvelled at the world through its ethical sourcing policies. The Group clearly outlines the code of conduct for all its suppliers to which they must strictly adhere. Part of its success stories is the use of third-party metrics from leading organizations like the United Nations Human Development Index and the International Labor Association to assess the ethics and quality of the businesses from where it sources its product components.

The Group's corporate social responsibility report also clearly states efforts required to improve energy efficiency in production, reduce water use, and packaging waste, etcetera.

Corporate social responsibility permits consumers to have an in-depth perspective on the ethics of the Group's sourcing processes while also becoming knowledgeable about its suppliers.

B. Starbucks

This frontline coffee manufacturing behemoth adopts a system known as C. A. F. E (Coffee and Farmer Equity Practices) in its manufacturing processes to improve sustainable coffee sourcing. With its 100% commitment to sustainably sourced coffee, the company is credited with strategically having four foundational core values or ideas that shape its business operations. These values are:

- Economic transparency
- Social responsibility
- Quality
- Environmental leadership

Economic Transparency

Here we see business ethics boldly given its place in business transactions. Starbucks' commitment to financial transparency reveals its position on business ethics and financial transactions. The coexistence of honest business practices and result-oriented systems promotes organizational excellence.

Social Responsibility: This takes us back to the convergence principle I explained in the hybrid system organizational process. Social responsibility values reveal your organization's commitment to human capital development.

The needs of people, communities and organizations around you should be areas of concern with actionable plans to address these challenges. Organizations that have business ethics factor in demography needs while fix their gaze on corporate goals.

Quality: Quality means a prime value or excellence. Quality distinguishes mediocre. Great ethical business practices consider quality as the engine of their products or services. Starbucks' relevance in coffee production is a result of the non-compromise of quality.

Environmental Leadership: Considerations of business activities and their impact on the planet are ethical business practices.

The damage done to our environment through human and business activities has resulted in devastating conditions like climate change where human and animal populations as well as plant life are being continually threatened and some plunged into extinction already.

Environmental pollution also plays a major role in public health implications. For instance, fumes or soot released by manufacturing companies can affect air quality, which poses significant health problems to exposed populations. Starbucks' environmental leadership demonstrates its great obligation to protect our environment while making the most amazing coffee on the planet.

C. Patagonia

This American clothing company has maintained its use of organically grown cotton for all its products since changing the pesticide-heavy cotton crops. The outdoor clothing company has built a resilient reputation for ethical practices through an environmentally compliant and ethical sourcing policy. The Patagonia brand has grown in leaps and bounds, resulting in a lot of patronages.

Additionally, its health insurance and paid paternity and maternity leave for its employees are ethical score points that give the brand dominance in outdoor clothing manufacturing in the world.

Many other organizations around the world are adopting ethical business models for their operations. The more you apply business ethics in your organization, the greater your chances of providing excellent products or services and spawning great visibility for your brand.

Why is Business Ethics Important for your Organization?

Many reasons exist why this significant area is vital for leading your organization or executing your tasks towards excellence. A few of these reasons are:

- Business ethics absolves your organization from corporate chaos.
- Provides moral guidelines as a compass for business operations.
- Prolongs the life of businesses.
- Builds trust and ease of doing business.
- Consolidates past successes through institutionally aimed reports from clients and reinforces future endorsements.

Absolution from Corporate Chaos

Every time business ethics are violated, either as an individual or as an organization, confusion often grips the person or business involved. The primary focus shifts from the goals of the organization and energy are dispersed across insignificant areas like staving off law enforcement agencies or regulatory financial misappropriation bodies.

You would lose your sleep over misconduct trials. The peace of your loved ones and employees through uninvited invasion of their private lives will be lost. Additionally, distorted views of the media will also leave permanent scars on your brand.

An online search with a negative brand reputation,

decades down the line, is not something you would want to play with. The effects of bad image travel unimaginable distances and damage reputations. All this chaos can be avoided from ground zero if business ethics are considered while starting or running an organization.

Chaos is a deal breaker. The moment investors smell disorder, especially morally disturbing problems in your business, they back out and distance themselves from taking up ventures that will taint their reputations and ruin the value of their investment in your organization.

Provision of Moral Guidelines as a Moral Compass for Business Operations

Guiding principles are crucial for excellent business execution at all levels. As enticing as face value is, clients will desert organizations without solid moral codes.

New business opportunities will evade corporations with weak or non-existent moral rules.
Some organizations with credible verifiable products or services at the front have been linked to drug rings and human trafficking activities and shady engagements at the back end.

For example, some development partners have institutional disclosure processes and policies that assess participation or non-engagement of organizations in activities revolving around firearms possession, child molestation, human trafficking and other related criminal activities.

Any trace of involvement in one or any of these activities automatically severs opportunities to access grants for intervention projects. This is how serious this gets, and businesses can also forfeit access to funding for social enterprise causes if they commit any of these crimes.

Business ethics helps your organization align to morally governing principles that result in corporate excellence. A steady rise in institutional excellence can change the trajectory of your business for good. A decline in excellence also significantly affects the downward trajectory of your organization. Business ethics or its negligence determines the direction of the impact your organization finds itself.

Prolongs the Life of Businesses
Just like products have their respective shelf lives, organizations also have a corporate lifespan. Some lose their relevance in a year; others stick through for five years, and a handful make it through a decade while generational businesses like Kellogg's are still evolving years after their founders are long gone.

Kellogg's is presently the most preferable breakfast brand all around the world. In 2019, the company was named one of the year's World's Most Ethical Companies by Ethisphere for the 11th time.

The well-articulated ethical performance culture of the company is visible on their website. Below is the statement from Kellogg's that captures this.

"W.K. Kellogg has given us a rich legacy of integrity and honouring that legacy has been a significant part of Kellogg Company's success story. Our Global Code of Ethics and K Values™ preserve our enduring commitment to integrity by shaping our ethical performance culture and by providing clear guidance, so our employees and stakeholders know where we stand and how we conduct business globally. Both demonstrate our unwavering commitment to doing business the right way-the Kellogg way."

The company's **Global Code of Ethics** is also translated for its growing customers in more than thirteen languages. What a way to preserve the legacy of Will Keith Kellogg, the founder of the Kellogg brand whose influence has spanned generations. Sustained ethical principles and their adherence can change the trajectory of your organization; thus, preserving the legacies you hold dear and prolonging the life of your business.

Business ethics can have an astronomical effect on your organization. I have used the diagram below to illustrate what this looks like.

Jamie Business Ethics Impact Graph
Business ethics and its impact can travel through successive generations when organizational leadership

understands and executes it through its business dealings. Always be ethically sensitive in your policies and processes as a business.

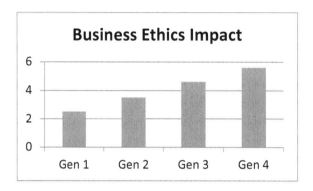

X-axis = the increase in business ethics over the generations.
Y-axis = the increase in market penetration over time where 1=100million.

Builds Trust & Ease of Doing Business

Ease of doing business does not always have to come from the part of governments. I believe it is a two-sided approach to sustainable business development.

If enabling policies are in place by the government, persons and organizations will still default basic rules that ensure beneficial business practices are achieved within the stipulated laws of that society. You have a major role to play in providing environments where business activities are done with ease. One such role is being **business ethics sensitive**.

An awareness of business ethics provides acceptable and unacceptable business conduct, thereby setting measurable expectations for business operations. One of the purposes of business ethics is to check irresponsibility. This awareness also promotes appropriate recognition and reward to employees and organizations making sustained efforts in remaining sensitive to the ethical rules of conducting business.

Trust issues are very slippery; they can crash an organization built 100 years back. Customers that trust your products or services can also serve as mouthpieces that drive active promotions for your organization. Every single action can build or destroy an institutional reputation. It is your job to protect everything worth the effort.

I am sure you will feel pained watching your years of smart work go down the drain. It takes a long process to build any structure. It can take just a few minutes to demolish a sky-rise building. This is what building and losing trust look like.

A beautiful architectural masterpiece can come crumbling in a matter of seconds-especially utilizing advanced demolition techniques.

Certain waves of organizational chaos can fold a thriving business. Losing trust as a business is one of the harshest places to find your organization. Do not let this happen before you learn the lessons the hard way.

Consolidates Past Successes Through Institutionally Aimed Reports.

Nothing beautifies business-like great reviews. Have you planned a trip from your home country and while making hotel reservation decisions, decide to spend some more time checking out reviews of the facilities you want to stay in?

Companies crave positive reviews of their products or services. It forms the basis with which they drive aggressive promotions. They even have packages for repeat customers that review their businesses.

Institutionalized reports aimed at businesses from clients support past business success stories while reinforcing future endorsements. It is every organization's dream. Consistent execution of excellence brings your organization to this point where your dreams unfold right in front of you, and yes, you can shed tears when this happens. This time, you will not cry the tears of pain, despair, and losses, but tears of joy, relevance and dogged commitment to excellence despite the levels of compromise of competitors.

Everyone appreciates a badge of honour. Organizations do too! The institutionalized appraisal can serve as a soundboard where the traditional values of your organization echo through generations.

However, to keep these reports flooding your space, here are some actions to take to preserve the beautiful stories that your products or services tell.

- Never compromise quality.
- Make excellence your personal and corporate identity.
- Honour employee efforts.
- Accept the pains of difference.

Never Compromise Quality
There are mistake thresholds that employees should not cross. It is okay to make one or two slips on duty. Reduce these mistakes through internship opportunities before actual employment. Do not tolerate any personal or institutional compromise on quality. You will be out of business if you do so.

Make Excellence your Personal & Corporate Identity
Excellence is like a nametag! People will see it a mile away. Your brand should be synonymous with excellence. A great way to make this happen is to develop an excellence policy and follow through with

all the resources at your disposal. I have a quick question for you: What do you want people to remember your organization for? I expect different answers to this question.

Follow me closely. At the core of whatever you want to be remembered for, add excellence as toppings. Have you had a yummy cup of ice cream before? Did the rich centre-filled toppings that decorated that cup of iced goodness sway you? People will most likely see your level of excellence first before they worry about what is in the cup.

Honour Employee Efforts

This shows up again! People, people and people are your true wealth. Do you want to become an excellent person? Observe excellent people! Do you want to birth excellent ideas? Hang around, excellent people! Do you dream about building an excellent organization? Study excellent institutions! Do you want your employees to execute high-end levels of excellence? Provide excellent systems and honour their efforts excellently! Human capital development is never a waste of resources.

Accept the Pains of Difference

Excellence has a price—**the price of difference**. The price for growth comes with the pains of difference. Some of the prices your organization must pay to get to the place of excellence are the prices of difference, the price of rejection and the price of separation. You need to know from inception that you have to be different to be able to achieve mind-blowing excellence in your business.

The difference comes with pain. You will need to delay certain levels of initial gratification to achieve excellence. You will also need a lot of maturities to understand your journey because no two organizations are the same, even when they sell the same products or provide similar services.

Understanding your difference puts you at a vantage point towards unusual levels of excellence. Now that you have understood the numerous strategies for executing excellence in your organization, I will need you to put these lessons into action plans. Develop a work plan and ways you can apply the things you have learned in your organization.

Last, I would love to be a part of your journey and guide you through the numerous hurdles of becoming a person of excellence, developing excellent systems and processes as well as building excellent organizations.

I strongly believe this book has offered relatable perspectives and suggestions for building one of the world's most excellent brands—*you*! I am also confident strong institutions will be the result of your commitment to personal excellence and the lessons you have learned in this book.

You are a brand, and your processes should be excellent. You are a voice, be excellence-driven. You matter, be the change. Let the journey begin! See you at the pinnacle of excellence!

If your work cannot speak for you when you are not there, then you do not have a voice. This is primarily due to two reasons.

First, organizational culture is significantly correlated with employee behaviour and attitude. Second, the ultimate creators of quality products and services are people, not technology.

Quality begins and ends with the individual because quality people do quality work. People manage processes and make the systems work; processes do not do work, people do. It is people who make poor systems work and good systems fail. In short, quality is the expression of human excellence.

Successful and enduring organizations have a culture that creates and sustains a work environment that is conducive to long-lasting quality improvement. According to Crosby, "Quality is the result of a carefully constructed culture; it has to be the fabric of the organization".

Organizational culture mirrors common views about "the way things are done around here." It is the "social glue" that binds an organization's members together and may be considered to be the personality of the organization.

Organizational culture is important for numerous reasons.

1. Organizational culture increases employee commitment and loyalty because of a sense of pride

and emotional attachment to certain core values.

2. It enables the attainment of strategic goals when there is a "fit" between culture and strategies. The success of any strategy rests heavily on the existence of supporting culture.

3. It facilitates decision-making by reducing disagreements about which premises should prevail since there is a greater sharing of beliefs and values.

4. It saves time as it spells out how people are to behave most of the time.

5. It facilitates communications since the employees speak a "common language". Shared values provide clues to help interpret messages.

6. Organizational culture provides meaning and purpose to work.

It is important to note that there can be no sustainable change without a change in employees' mindsets. Organizations do not adapt to change, people do.

In the words of Black and Gregersen, "Lasting success lies in changing individuals first; then the organization follows. An organization changes only as far or as fast as its collective individuals change."

Any initiative to improve quality is unlikely to succeed unless it is embedded in and reflected by the culture of the organization. Also, if total quality improvement efforts are inconsistent with the organizational culture, the efforts will be undermined. Quality is not evangelism, suggestion boxes, or slogans. It is a way of life. Based upon successful cultural transformation efforts and literature review, there are numerous strategies for making quality a way of life in an organization.

First, top management must demonstrate visible commitment and explicit involvement in efforts aimed at embedding quality into the basic fabric of everyday organizational life. Senior managers must personally lead cultural transformation efforts and reinforce the new organizational culture through word and deed.

In the words of Thomson and Strickland, "Only top management has the power and organizational influence to bring about major cultural change."

Similarly, Kotter and Heskett state that competent leadership is the single most visible factor that distinguishes major cultural changes that succeed from those that fail. Towards this end, quality should be integrated into the organization's mission statement and corporate philosophy.

For example, as the CEO of Vantage Group, I established and modelled three basic values that represent the core of Vantage Group's organizational culture:
- Respect for the individual.
- Service to our customers.
- Striving for excellence.

Top management should allocate adequate resources

for quality improvement and establish corporate quality goals and measure progress towards attaining them regularly, participate in training and be accessible to employees and customers.

Second, leaders must model the desired behaviour. Employees watch the top leaders for signals about what matters and what does not. People learn by observation and are likely to emulate those behaviours that they believe are likely to lead to success. Leaders should convey clear and consistent signals about desired values and norms through their behaviours (what they say and do).

Third, top management needs to foster a climate of mutual trust and teamwork, which is crucial for creating and sustaining a quality culture. In this regard, top managers should honour promises and commitments; maintain open and honest communication; avoid the formation of cliques or subgroups; encourage the free flow of information; establish cross-functional teams, and encourage discussion of key problems and issues.

Fourth, management should recruit new people (including key positions) that are compatible with the desired quality culture. For example, they show potential employees a video in which the company's values are succinctly explained. Understanding these values help people screen themselves before they sign up.
Organizations can also utilize personality

questionnaires and interest inventories in selecting staff that will conform to the desired culture.

Organizational core values can be reinforced further through orientation or socialization programs. For example, Disney World has a two-day orientation program where every new employee meets Walt Disney (through videotapes) and learns about his vision and core values, including treating every customer as a "guest" and every employee as a "performing artist".

New Sanyo employees go through an intensive five-month program where they learn the Sanyo way of doing things—from how to speak to superiors to proper grooming and dressing. Some organizations also utilize stories or legends to remind everyone of the organization's core values and what they mean.

Fifth, management should provide appropriate training and other supports that permit employees to embrace the new culture and to fully understand quality principles. The entire workforce needs to acquire new knowledge, skills and attitudes. Every employee must clearly understand his or her role in making quality happen. Training sessions must start with top management and cascade down the organization.

Quality training should cover quality awareness, basic quality concepts and tools, process management, communication skills, interpersonal skills, problem-solving skills, and team building. Organizations noted for world-class quality typically devote 40-80 hours per year, per person to training.

Sixth, employees at all levels must be engaged, be involved, and take ownership of the cultural change. Participation in the cultural change process tends to reduce resistance to change besides enhancing both satisfaction and employee productivity. In this regard, gaining the support of middle managers at the department or divisional level is crucial.

Management should get them involved in designing and promoting quality improvement efforts. Decision-making authority should be pushed down to the lowest possible level. Teamwork should be promoted through the establishment of steering committees, cross-functional teams and quality circles.

Seventh, incorporating core values in the performance management system should reinforce the desired quality culture and base rewards on meeting quality goals and demonstrating appropriate behaviour (besides technical competence). Who gets promoted says more about real values than any mission statement.

Eighth, management should use every vehicle possible (including conferences, videos, posters, and in-house magazines) to communicate organizational direction, key values and quality achievements by employees. According to Kotter, "Without credible communication, and a lot of it, employees' hearts and minds are never captured."

Conclusively, creating and sustaining a quality culture that facilitates continuous change and improvement is crucial for long-term organizational success. Changing organizational culture is a challenging and time-consuming process because it necessitates changes in the way people think and behave.

To ensure success, cultural change efforts must focus on formulating a clear, compelling and shared vision; securing sustained top management commitment; role modelling of desired behaviour by top leaders; promoting employee involvement and empowerment; conducting appropriate training at all levels to imbibe the quality culture; maintaining open and honest communication; fostering a climate of trust and collaboration; and embedding cultural changes in the organization's structure, systems and policies. It is important to ensure that the desired quality culture is compatible with organizational strategy.

A great part of business ethics and excellence is developing a system of quality improvement. In the pages that follow, I will carefully clarify what this entails.

Chapter 11: Developing a System of Quality Improvement

You are considered a professional when you get paid to play music. When people hire us, they expect quality. There are no excuses. Not being prepared is simply not an option.

People do not pay for average. Would you pay for an average meal, movie, book, concert, cell phone or computer? People pay for quality and excellence.

Providing quality products and services that delight customers are crucial for ensuring long-term organizational success in today's highly competitive and rapidly changing world. In this regard, creating and sustaining a "quality culture" is a prerequisite for ensuring a continuous flow of quality products and services.

Every leader that will cause a transformational change in the twenty-first century needs to cultivate the mindset of global thinking. We will never execute excellence without thinking about quality. The world currently needs local content, presented in a globally acceptable way.

Excellence will push you to explore innovative pathways to getting your products or services out there without compromising product or service quality. In the business world where many businesses and organizations cut corners to keep their heads above the water, the most priceless commodity right now is **quality**.

- Quality of personnel
- Quality of systems & processes
- Quality of products and/or services
- Quality of service

I listed these in their order of importance and will explain why this is so as you closely follow me.

Quality of Personnel
Your impact as an organization will be driven by people at the backend no matter the level of automation that happens on the front end. The person you bring on board will either bury or build your organization. The quality of personnel is central to the overall vision of your organization and business.

Poor recruitment decisions can cost you a fortune—the

loss of credibility and low productivity levels on all fronts. Skill is as important as academic qualifications. In the heat of the storm, where knowledge is tested, the skill will always win as I have seen people spend years in academic institutions and cannot solve problems in their fields!

Whom do you call when machines malfunction or processes become difficult to assimilate? Who saves you from poor investment decisions? Who challenges your organization's adherence to ISO standards? Who does your risk assessment? Who provides counsel and helps you avoid corporate sharks and legal landmines? These questions will be answered by the quality of personnel in your organization.

Quality of Systems & Processes

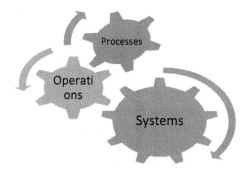

Organizational POS Model

Systems and processes are the engine rooms of your operations as a business or organization. The day-to-day activities within your business can be seamless or difficult through the availability or absence of systems and processes that make operations easy and efficient. The quality of these systems can tell if you have a global or local mindset. You can be a local business, but you should strive to be global in your operations.

This brings you to a place where you can comfortably compete with businesses in advanced climes even when running a local business in a struggling economy. Quality systems and processes optimize performance and simplify tasks that would normally require enormous amounts of time.

What differentiates organizations A from B is their systems and processes. Further measurement of this divide is the **quality of their systems.** Never settle for less or compromise your way through. Systems and processes are the moulds that provide remarkable excellence in cutting-edge organizations around the world. Your ability to evolve with the current developments in the business world is tied to your systems and structures as an organization.

Quality of Products and/or Services

Global thinking prompts you to consider these quality levels in your organization. Have you ever walked into a beautiful office with poor service? Have you ordered a product online and received an entirely different quality from what you ordered?

Have you bought a product and it gets broken in a few

hours? Or, paid for a service and became full of rage after the quality of delivery?

Possible occurrences like this reveal the quality of a product or service of any business. It could be very painful when such things happen. Your mind quickly runs through the list of product or service options you have.
As much as the affected business tries to carry out damage control, the impression of quality provision has been dented among customers. It is the same thing with service-based businesses or organizations.

When quality is compromised, damage control does not easily erase clients' negative impressions. Automobile and aircraft companies have had to recall their products over repeated crashes. Lives have been lost over collapsed buildings. Buildings have been set ablaze over inferior electrical wiring products. These errors point back to quality compromise.

Sometimes, the damage lasts a lifetime. Businesses with quality improvement and quality assurance policies seldom have these problems. Executing excellence comes in all shades of demands and quality compromise cannot be allowed to replace excellence.

Quality of products and services can tie generational client bonds. Compromise of quality can severe these loyalties. Nothing beats personal connections. When a customer loves your product, one of the strategies for repeat sales or services is product or service quality.

Personal connections to quality products and services do not easily change until quality compromise sneaks in. You will never lose a client whose quality preference has been consistently met.

Quality of Service

You can have a wonderful product with terrible service. Poor service delivery is one of the reasons why products outlive their shelf lives. Your customer care personnel cannot risk being harsh to a customer over the phone. We have seen a front desk officer in a 5-star hotel in Atlanta fisticuffing with a client.

My car should not be in a poorer state after leaving your workshop with attractive signage. A school should not leave a student more confused about the art of inquiry, exploration and interrogation.

Quality enhances longevity! Have you ever had a pair of shoes that will not just get worse? Sometimes, it travels two generations or more. As hilarious as this may sound, there are companies whose primary objective is creating footwear memories. Quality makes this possible. Never compromise quality! Quality is the difference between two businesses in the same industry.

I would rather go for the price of one quality product than repeat purchases of inferior products at cheap prices. I will spend more money on the latter eventually and still be plagued with terrible user experience. I am sure you can see the difference staring at you right here. If you are allowed to choose between quality and compromise, choose the former!

There will be situations of quality compromise flying around you whether you are starting or an already existing business. It may be inflation, low sales, rent troubles, policy challenges etc. Each of these problems mentioned here and many more do not permanently damage corporate reputation like a quality compromise. You will find yourself in a very difficult position to build back trust.

Things Quality Will Afford Your Business or Organization

- Sales
- More Sales
- Unbelievable Turnover
- Client Loyalty

Sales

Sales are much easier when you have continuously sustained product or service quality. This, however, does not mean you should lower your promotional activities. It gets to a point where quality becomes your promotion and people begin to attribute your organization to excellence. This does not happen with the speed of light; it takes years of smart work, research on evolving preferences, and strategy, to bring tons of excellence to the table.

Competing favourably in your business industry requires a careful understanding of market segmentation and excellence-driven execution. The basis for being in business is solving problems. Sales help you solve these problems! And, you cannot make sustained sales without quality.

More Sales

Have you ever consumed a product for the first time and immediately ordered more? You quickly remember your colleagues may crave this product and your spouse may lose an arm having tried it. Sounds hilarious, right? Quality makes this happen. What unscrews individual A's nuts may not loosen individual Bs' nuts. Quality is individual-centric, but can never be ignored.

Repeat sales or purchases keep businesses afloat. No matter the serene looks of your office or the jaw-dropping facility that houses your organization, sales or services must be happening. Quality makes more sales possible. Quality sustains excellence and when adequately executed; a lifetime of wealth creation becomes possible.

Unbelievable Turnover

Businesses can have more sales but be left with depleted turnover. Quality affords you a steady rise in revenue while meeting the needs of the people you serve. On the other hand, compromising on quality gradually depletes your earnings as resources are sunk into damage control, legal battles and image-saving endeavours.

Continuous quality control is a strategic game plan for innovative corporations that have visionary leaders. It can also be said that the level of revenue your organization handles is directly proportional to the quality level of your products or services. Therefore, it can be said that the level of product or service quality equals the amount of business turnover.

Client Loyalty

I have a friend who will never drive anything but a Mercedes-Benz. As wonderful and economically friendly as Toyota products are, he has an amazing allegiance to the German manufacturer.

I have made several attempts to talk him into trying another automobile brand, but his convictions are **'not negotiable'** (his words). I laugh hard when this phrase pops out of him. Amazingly, his spouse and children, too, have developed an undying passion for Mercedes-Benz products. This is how quality floors compete for products.

What are those things you can incorporate into your brand that will distinguish it from the sea of products out there? Make that a part of your brand story and watch client loyalty shoots up your business to an enviable height.

Chapter 12: Human Factor Compliance

The ability to design experiences that take people, machines, and workplace behaviour into consideration is one of the significant processes for executing excellence in your organization. This is simply known as ergonomics or human factors.

The world has changed forever and the ease at which organizations do business has changed forever. The most endearing processes are people-centred. Building an organization that isolates humans, their behaviour and their engagements is a recipe for organizational disaster.

The level of ease, comfort and forward-thinking

currently present in organizations across the world announces heightened competition across all sectors. Whether you are a software start-up, a local farm, a cleaning firm, or a veterinary service, human factors compliance with your products or services will bring cutting-edge levels of excellence to the problems you solve.

With comfort on the priority list of clients, you can never dodge this except if you want to compete locally. Local competition is fine at lower levels; however, if you want to become a high-performance organization with excellent results, you should never downplay safety, comfort and ease.

What is Ergonomics?

According to the International Ergonomics Association (IEA), ergonomics is the scientific discipline concerned with the understanding of interactions among humans and other elements of a system, and the profession that applies theory, principles, data and methods to design to optimize human well-being and overall system performance.

This might sound a bit technical; but simply means the connection between what you do, how you do it and the relationship between machines and humans while doing what you do. This connection helps you think about human and workplace safety first before designing your products and/or services.

This word is credited to have Greek origins from

"ergon" meaning work and **"nomos"** meaning laws. So, contextually and in very clear terms, you could say designing laws that guide workplace safety and ultimately, performance. It is broadly categorized into three domains:

- Physical
- Cognitive
- Organizational

Physical Ergonomics

This area of ergonomics focuses on the human structural, anthropometric (bodily measurements), and physiological and biomechanical features as they relate to physical activity. So, an aircraft has doors that any body size can pass through.

Also, buildings have standardized accessibility plans that make habitation or use comfortable about the purpose for which the structure was designed.

Cognitive Ergonomics

This area of ergonomics focuses on mental processes such as perception, memory, reasoning, and motor response as they affect connections between humans and other components of a system.

For example, if I am sure skydiving with the right apparatus will be a memorable experience because of the durability of the kit, I can comfortably make safety associations of the kit with the memorable experience I am looking forward to.

This means if a skydiving kit company passes the durability test of their products, they most likely will get a loyal customer in me for life.

The safety design-thinking approach of this company will guide the development of every product in this organization. What this means is that they are simply selling safety and memories. Thus, if I can make these associations before I make the first product purchase, they have leveraged cognitive ergonomics to get their products out in the market.

Organizational Ergonomics
This area of ergonomics focuses on the optimization of sociotechnical systems, including organizational structures, policies and processes. Now, taking the skydiving kit company as a further example, developing policies and building systems that check human connections with these products are strategies for achieving organizational ergonomics.

The relatability of these three areas is seen clearly in human connections to products or services. However, you have to know what area of ergonomics your product or services most likely leverages to provide an adequate excellent user experience for your business.

As an organization with a global vision, it is particularly important you consider human factors compliance as one of the components in your arsenal of strategies for corporate growth. Human factors compliance benefits your organization on all fronts. It incorporates all possible domains in providing all-around comfort for your customers.

Why Human Factor Compliance Matters in Your Organization

Many things are important for your organization. However, many of them do not matter! For example, having a series of debriefing meetings over a product that has resulted in unprecedented levels of discomfort for customers is futile. Regardless of the level of excellence, you want to achieve, majoring in a minor can cost you time, resources and energy.

Moreover, focusing on **majors** sets every other thing in place. An ergonomics policy can solve possible futuristic occurrences of the discomfort mentioned in the lines above. I consider human factors compliance a **major** that makes excellent execution possible in all the units, departments and cadre of your organization. Here are a few ways why you should consider human factors compliance in your organization.

- It lowers cost.
- It creates a safety culture.
- Improves employee engagement.
- Results in high productivity and high performance.
- Results in better product or service quality.

Lowers Cost
Do not make the mistake most organizations do— reviewing pitfalls after financial resources have gone down the drain. Risk assessment is one of the processes

of ergonomics. For example, human factor compliance helps your organization check for possible Musculoskeletal Disorder (MSD) risk factors associated with your product or service use.

MSDs are injuries and disorders that affect the human body's movement or a musculoskeletal system like nerves, blood vessels, muscles, tendons, ligaments, discs, etcetera. Your organization may never recover from legal battles (especially in developed nations) when evidence proves your products or services lead to mild or severe cases of MSD.

Common MSDs include carpal tunnel syndrome, muscle and tendon strain, and tendonitis.
Issues like these can land a negligent company in shark-infested legal waters. Human Factor compliance helps you not to get drowned in the first place, thereby reinforcing your organization's commitment to institutional excellence.

It lowers the cost of hiring expensive lawyers to defend your organization in court and reduces capital expenditures on products and services that do not align with human-centred design.

Safety Culture
It is always saddening to see organizations put the safety of their employees and customers last while making products, services and sales their top priority. This happens particularly when policies that enforce human factors are non-existent within such

organizations. I am sure you have heard the phrase "Safety First" uncountable times.

The confidence clients have in your products or services is primarily because they are safe. If I perceive my consumption or use of a product or service as a threat to my physical or mental health, I will immediately discontinue its use.

Guess what? Human Factor compliance will not allow your products or services to get to this point. It puts the necessary measures in place and checks both individual and organizational safety.

Improves Employee Engagement
Interaction between colleagues in job roles can never be more fun and engaging when processes are integrated with human relations and experience. The workflow and camaraderie between employers and employees are remarkable.

Human Factors compliance gets you an amazing relational ticket with your team. It shows your understanding of their needs, work environment, and thoughtfulness about their health on duty and that you increasingly value their presence and the effort they put in place to help you run an excellence-driven organization.

These affordances can encourage them to stand as guarantors for their relatives to have job roles in your organization. This means they can stake their reputation on the line for your organization. What goodwill can be better than this? This action projects many things. I will name a few.

- Listening culture in your organization.
- Opinion-sharing opportunities.
- Interaction mindedness.

Organizational Listening Culture

Many employers lack social competence and pay little or no attention to their employees' suggestions. Do not fall into this trap. It spells doom and the gradual collapse of your organization.

Give a listening ear when suggestions that will add value to the organization are brought to you regardless of personal differences between you and your subordinates. It could save your organization from trouble. Listeners are learners! Help your organization by becoming a great learner. Listen! Listen again!! Listen more!!!

Opinion Sharing Opportunities

Opinions shape organizations. As long as you have a team, each of them has opinions that you should always respect. Ask them what they feel and think about certain issues or projects within your organization. Opinion sharing will give you leverage over competitors.

Your employees may make silent social observations for long periods concerning your operations, documentation, development planning, etcetera. Their ability to be assertive and confidently express how they feel regarding the areas that matter to them and the overall development of your organization is an excellent atmosphere that you must create.

Recommendations, lapses of competitors and their success strategies are shared during opinion-sharing sessions. Make your employees look forward to these sessions.

Interaction Mindedness
This is an overflow from opinion sharing opinion-sharing opportunities. Your team's freedom to expressly share their views fosters interaction and possible scale-up options for your organization. For example, when your automobile is adequately oil-gauged, it gives your engine the freedom to drive maximum performance.

This is like giving your employees the freedom to share their perspectives. It unearths the truth, minimizes future errors and results in the expansion of your business. Only intentional, institutional-driven conversations make this happen. Learn to further conversations. Allow your team to create further brainstorming sessions that will engage their minds.

The beautiful part of this is when enduring solutions are birthed in the place of organized conversations; excellence is achieved through a constant result-oriented engagement process.

High Productivity & Performance
Human Factors compliance largely contributes to

increased productivity and organizational performance. Successful institutions periodically review their ergonomics policies. This enables them to make appropriate decisions and adjustments necessary for increased downlines. Environments and conditions where employees' safety is taken into maximum consideration become avenues for tremendous productivity levels.

Here is the catch. Productivity and performance can be measured. If you are doing well as an organization, it will show. If you are doing badly, it will be glaring as well. You can never be excellent without being productive. Productivity is the reward for excellence. Let us take a closer look at how productivity helps you execute excellence in your organization.

Productivity & Excellence
High-tech developments, globalization, and ever-increasing client expectations are significant factors that have increased high productivity needs for businesses and corporate institutions.

How well your organization can convert **input** such as (machines, labour and materials) into products and services or **output** is the incredible process of productivity. Considering that the world is changing rapidly, working smarter is not only necessary but also gradually becoming a requirement to remain relevant as a business.

You cannot afford to adopt obsolete methods in

running a twenty-first-century-compliant business. The losses will be monumental. Interestingly, you can start small and ensure excellence all through your baby steps. The future of work revolves around technology, the digital economy and human capital development.

You will shoot yourself in the legs if you ignore these areas. Human Factor compliance aligns with these areas and makes productivity and high performance achievable. Every step along the way will test your adherence to ergonomics and it is possible to have a great vision ruined with bad methods. Homegrown excellence is not an event; it is a process.

I recommend you look for opportunities to increase excellence and productivity in your organization. A few areas to consider are:

- Use of the right tools or equipment.
- Utilize technology to improve operations.
- Review your organizational setup.
- Implement continuous improvement methods.

Use the Right Tools

The wrong tools will keep your entire organization on a spot. Human Factors compliance will help you make smart decisions on tools procurement. Use of the wrong tools can recalibrate your efforts backwards and short-circuit opportunities for productivity, excellence and growth. The right tools will optimize your operations, increase efficiency and engage your employees.

It will also place demands on daily personal development where skills would need to be upgraded to utilize advanced tools for increased productivity. Ergonomics facilitates smart decisions and results in choices that benefit organizations exponentially. The use of the right tools will achieve the following:

- Reduce cost
- Save time
- Smart work
- Corporate creativity
- Employee motivation
- High productivity & increased performance

Cost Reduction

Organizations want to cut costs while maintaining their product or service standards. Reducing non-essential expenditures is one of the advantages of human factors compliance.

The amount of financial resources businesses waste on product designs, procurements and services where ergonomics is discounted is sickening.

Many organizations do not recover from these mistakes. You can choose to have your costs cut by adopting human factors approach in your business or bury your organization through negligence. The first saves cost and the latter increase cost.

Time-Saving

Have you ever played a game and kept flouting game rules? Repeated violations of game rules will get you back on ground zero—the whole time. The time you would use to progress to advanced levels will slip through your hands as you have to learn to navigate the basics of the first phase. At the end of it all, you will lose a lot of time. The good side of this negligence is that you can repeat trials as many times as possible while learning the ropes of the game.

In organizational development, you do not play games instead you apply principles. There are mistakes you make that invite the full wrath of the law. No one trails you when you goof on games! Human factors compliance saves jail time, reduces the cost of non-essential labour, results in efficiency and removes drudgery challenges that kill time.

Smart Work

Hard work will rob your team of their physical strength and shorten their lifespan. Smart thinking and smart work have replaced toiling. Hard work is a wonderful core value to have as a business; however, the world is run by smart systems. The processes of these systems are overhauled and optimized to drive excellence in a matter of seconds.

You will never be at par with forward-thinking organizations if you do not work smart. Today, we see drones deployed to deliver medical supplies to military troops, thereby eliminating more human deaths. We are already in a generation of driverless cars. Working smart takes deliberate effort to upset normalcy, break rules and alter ideologies with superior products and services.

Human factors compliance helps organizations to achieve this. For example, many high schools and universities globally are becoming EMIS-Smart schools. EMIS is an acronym for E-Learning Management Information Systems. Students can now have a blended learning experience from the comfort of their homes. EMIS platforms combine physical, mental, social and organizational aspects of ergonomics in providing high-level education affordances for students.

Corporate Creativity
Corporate creativity is a by-product of sustained levels of organizational excellence. Innovation and ingenuity come alive when ergonomics are factored into product or service design and development. This also results in institutionalized reports aimed at an organization.

Over the years, Airbus has gradually built a global brand that brings an incredible reputation to the aircraft and the company. The company's adherence to human factors has given them global recognition in aircraft assembling through their dogged compliance with ergonomics.
Always strive for creativity in your organization. Creative organizations are hubs of excellence.

Employee Motivation

The adrenaline that pumps the results we visibly see as **"excellence"** is staff motivation. Nothing you ever do should make you think excellence is achieved in isolation. It is a lie of the century! Every member of your team has an emotional bank account.

Every word of encouragement, pat on the back, thumbs up, a wide smile, etcetera, goes into these emotional accounts as deposits. Workplace ridicule, defamation, and deprivation also store up as deposits.

Making withdrawals will call up the deposits you have lodged over time. Employee motivation sets the tone for productivity and excellence. I am sure you have some knowledge about the GIGO (Garbage In, Garbage Out) process of computers.

The level of courage you pump into your employees will determine their level of commitment to their jobs and the organization. What goes into them, comes right back to you.

High Productivity & Increased Performance

I have written extensively on high-performance organizations and productivity in this book. I will add a little more colour to these areas and human factors compliance. Beginning from Small and Medium Enterprises (SMEs) to large corporations, excellence contributes greatly to high productivity and increased performance.

Budding catering service in a remote town and a long-standing twenty-first-century compliant software development company in a commercial city centre that adopts human factors may never get the same results, but each will achieve high productivity and increased performance at its level.

No matter your level as an organization, grow at your pace and organically. Apply consistent adherence to best practices in your industry, drive excellent systems and processes, review your organizational structure occasionally and watch your business achieve high-level productivity and increased performance at astronomical levels.

Utilize Technology to Improve Operations.
Technological advances such as nanotechnology are aiding improvements in several sectors like transportation, security, medical science, environment, information technology, and agriculture.

No matter the industry of your business, it is of primary importance to look out for present and future technology that will help drive corporate excellence in your organization. It is also noteworthy that failure to be tech-compliant may deprive your organization of the necessary opportunities required for high-end productivity.

Quality jobs can be done in a matter of seconds. Assembling and preparing these technologies may take time and sometimes years depending on your industry.

However, the goal is productivity, which will be driven by excellent execution of tasks, processes and systems.

Utilization of the right technology that improves operations remains a sustainable route to achieving this goal.

Routine operational activities without appropriate task-based technology can be boring, especially in supply chain-based companies. For example, the amount of time wasted on achieving a single task can export a product assembled with the right technology. Mechanization has helped agriculture beat traditional harvesting methods like handpicking ripened fruits.

Physical energies can be converted to more benefitting tasks like development planning and growth thinking. Leveraging technology can yield awesome rewards for your business if you can utilize the several tools available in your sector for maximum productivity.

Review Organizational Setup
You must run occasional structural checks to reveal institutional lapses. In the construction industry, the pressure test is run on building materials to ascertain their level of susceptibility to errors that can threaten human safety. Reviewing your organization's setup periodically will expose the practices, operations or policies that hinder efficiency.

Alterations of buildings must comply with regulatory approvals. This will require assessments and other precautionary measures that protect lives and property by the professionals in that field. In-house reviews are opportunities to uncover frameworks that prevent maximum productivity.

It is upon this premise that I strongly advise that you also leverage your Annual General Meetings (AGMs) to strategically review your business setup. Let your stakeholders know and bring to the fore the reasons for investing in the organization. Structural deficits can have long-term negative implications for your business.

You should not sacrifice the structural setup of the business while being swamped with the demands of protecting every investor's interests. Intermittent reviews, when foundational setup and cracks are checked, lead to excellent practices. It may cost you time, resources, and painful adjustments, but the benefits are enormous.

Implement Continuous Improvement Methods
Continuous improvement and excellence are two sides of a coin. No organization succeeds by flouting continuous improvement of its systems. An automobile will display a malfunction on its dashboard, which serves as a warning about an operational failure.

What amazes me more is that despite these signals, some drivers will disregard the prompts and still rev these vehicles for months! You know what awaits such road users, and frankly speaking, the results are always unpalatable.

On the flip side, regular automobile checks and appropriate maintenance (quality part replacements) can save your life, your passengers and other road users.

Let us apply this to your organization. Continuous improvement will not only save your organization financial ruin; it will keep putting food on the tables of your employees and solve the problems your business was incorporated to address. I

have a very reflective question for you at this point, who loses out over failed continuous improvement efforts? Your organization or your clients? Your guess is as good as mine!

As you focus on organizational excellence, below are a few ways continuous improvement can be regularized in your organization.

- Demand accountability.
- Have a continuous improvement team.
- Celebrate continuous improvement successes.
- Provide opportunities that help and support the team.

Authors Note.

Human factor compliance and many more continuous improvement methods can be adopted to drive organizational excellence. Interestingly, human compliance with personal values, business ethics, organizational goals and utilization of systems and processes makes excellence possible. It is upon this premise that every other thing falls into place. As you prepare to apply the things you have learned in this book, I hope that you align with the principles that make excellence achievable. Anything accomplished is worth executing excellently.

Let the journey begin!

CONTACT ME!

One thing I love most is receiving feedback from grateful readers whose lives and careers have been transformed by reading my book.

So, if you have enjoyed this book, or it has impacted your life and business, I will love to hear from you.

Send me your feedback through info@jamiepajoelinternational.org.

For Executive Leadership & Business Coaching, please contact:

CANADA OFFICE.
8, Highbrook Street, Kitchener, Ontario, Canada.
T: +1 5197212399
info@jamiepajoelinternational.org
www.jamiepajoelinternational.org

Made in the USA
Columbia, SC
01 December 2022

72464099R00100